LUTHER
and his
KATIE

DOLINA MacCUISH

LUTHER
and his
KATIE

*The Influence of Luther's
Wife on His Ministry*

**CHRISTIAN
FOCUS**

Dolina MacCuish is a retired school teacher who lives in Inverness. She is a keen biographer and enjoys researching historical figures. She has also written *Augustine, a Mother's Son*.

Copyright © Christian Focus Publications 1983
ISBN: 978-1-78191-967-5

First published in 1983
Reprinted in 1989, 1999 and 2017
by
Christian Focus Publications Ltd
Geanies House, Fearn, Ross-shire,
IV20 1TW, U.K.
www.christianfocus.com

Cover design by Pete Barnsley

Printed and bound by
Bell and Bain, Glasgow

CONTENTS

INTRODUCTION

At the famous Leipzig Disputation between Martin Luther and John Eck in 1519, which effectively pushed Luther out of the medieval church, everyone remarked that the monk from Wittenberg carried in his hand a bunch of flowers, in moments of pressure looking at them and enjoying their fragrance. Someone has aptly said that amid the storms and stresses of his later life Luther's wife and children were his bunch of violets.

Though Catherine von Bora without question owes her place in history to the fact that she was Luther's 'liebes Weib' yet she was noteworthy on her own account. Someone whom the volcano that was Luther could call 'lord Katie' ought not to be ignored. Indeed a German historian has gone so far as to wonder what Luther would have been without her. 'Was wäre Luther ohne seine Käthe?'

This book began with an interest in Catherine von Bora, but it soon became clear that one was seeing her through Luther's eyes in innumerable little references to her in his letters and conversation, and also in the context of his life. She was thus in a double sense 'his Katie'.

1

HANS' SON

In her old age Margaret Luther could tell Melancthon the hour (eleven at night) and the day on which her eldest son was born – but not the year! Such is the difference between a mother's interest and a biographer's. The year was 1483 and the place was the little town of Eisleben in Saxony. The house, partly burned, was restored in 1817 and bears the inscription;

'In this house Dr. Martin Luther was born, the 10th of November, 1483.

Christi Wort ist Luthers Lehr
Drum verghet sie nimmermehr.'

(Christ's own Word is Luther's lore,
And it remains for evermore.)

On the following day he was baptised in St Peter's Church and named after the saint whose festival it was.

Six months later Hans Luther took his family to Mansfeld six miles away in search of work. He came of peasant stock and, judging by Martin's later references to his peasant background, he retained much of its outlook. In actual fact, of course, he had come to Mansfeld to find work in the mines – mainly silver and copper – so that young Martin grew up in a mining community. There they were at first very poor and Hans and Margaret Luther were hard put to provide for their family which eventually numbered seven children, at least four of them boys. Years later Martin wrote, 'My father was a poor miner, and my mother often carried wood on her back; they worked the flesh off their bones to bring us up.' The intelligent, hard-working father eventually became quite prosperous acquiring one or two small foundries and becoming a councillor.

A hard, if not harsh, inflexible man he was very definitely master in his own household. Discipline was strict; there was no intention of spoiling the child for want of using the rod. And he was ambitious, especially for his oldest son whose exceptional abilities became early apparent. If education was the path to advancement then money was going to be found to give this first-born of his the best available. Like so many parents he was prepared to make sacrifices to give his son what he himself had lacked. Perhaps the poverty they experienced as a family was partly due to the need to put savings by for the children's education.

Hans was a short, stocky man with a strong-looking frame. Cranach's portrait of 1527 is full of life and character; it shows a strong, rugged face – the face of a man who has battled his way through life. The cheekbones are high, the eyes intelligent and clear-sighted, the mouth and chin determined. The work-toughened hands look ready for action.

His wife's portrait, by contrast, suggests mildness and long-suffering. The face is narrow and bony. The eyes with their far-away reflective gaze, the patient mouth and the reposing work-hardened hands all combine to give an impression of passivity. The mood is pensive, almost sombre. One is not surprised to learn that she was the more superstitious of the two. Martin recalled that she attributed to the witchery of a neighbour woman the deaths of several of her children in infancy. ('They cried themselves to death' is how he remembered it). Not much is known of her history beyond the fact that she was the daughter of a prosperous tradesman of Neustadt near Eisenach. Melancthon, who knew her in her old age, thought highly of her and spoke of her as a woman of prayer.

Martin's childhood, according to himself, was unhappy. The grinding poverty had something to do with it but what really burned into his soul was the severe discipline – especially his father's. Yet there was a strong bond between the two. On one occasion, after a beating, he went off fuming with resentment till his father was at pains to win him to himself again. Hard, unyielding Hans

11

did go out of his way to heal the breach – and young Martin noticed and remembered. He also remembered how his father would kneel by his bed at night to ask God's blessing on his little son.

His mother may not have been so harsh though she, too, could be very strict. He records how at one time she gave him such a beating for stealing a hazelnut that blood was drawn. Yet we must not read too much into that. There may have been ramifications to the incident which the young miscreant soon forgot while the 'one nut' still rankled. The fact that the occasion was remembered may indicate that it was rather exceptional. His mother must have been under considerable pressure what with her sizeable family, lack of money, ailing babies and her own state of health.

He had the consolation, however, of knowing they meant well. 'They seriously thought they were doing right, but they did not take differences of personality into account. This, however, is very necessary so that one may know when, and where, and how to inflict chastisement. It is necessary to punish; but the apple should be placed beside the rod.' Besides, such methods of discipline were general in his day which at least meant he was not the odd one out – all his friends were in the same boat. To add to his fears were the myriad fiends, witches, hobgoblins, demons and the like that leered from buildings, gateways and woodcuts and peopled the spiritual imagination of the time. What effect, one wonders, did the deaths of his baby brothers and sisters have on him? The upshot was that he grew up timid and fearful with a scrupulous, demanding conscience.

Yet there must have been fun too, with all these brothers and sisters. He remembers his mother singing to him and he certainly acquired a large repertoire of folk-songs. His memories of his mother gathering sticks in the forest may well have had overtones of pleasure. It was, in any case, a privilege the townspeople had and one can scarcely imagine a foray for firewood being other than purposeful and companionable.

Hans planned great things for his eldest son so off to school he went. The school was some distance away, too far for such a little fellow to walk so he had to be carried part of the way. Years later he wrote in the Bible of his sister's husband: 'To my good old friend, Nicholas Emler, who more than once carried me in his arms to school and back again when I was a little boy, neither of us then knowing that one brother-in-law was carrying another.' In this school besides Latin and some maths, he learned the Catechism, the Ten Commandments, the creed and the Lord's Prayer. He says, 'My religious instruction was imparted with the same severity as my secular; I turned pale and was terrified at the very name of Christ. I regarded Christ as nothing more than a strict and angry judge.' The week's tally of punishment was saved up for the last day and so it was that one Friday morning he had accrued fifteen whippings!

When he was fourteen he was moved to the Franciscan School at Magdeburg where he stayed one year. One or two memories from that time stood out. Christmas drew near and he went carol-singing with some friends from door to door. As they sang in front of one farmhouse standing by itself at the end of the village the farmer came out and called gruffly, 'Where are you boys?' They took to their heels, terrified. The farmer kept calling them till at last they went back – and gratefully took the sausages he proffered! It was there also he saw something he would never forget – the emaciated Prince William of Anhalt walking the streets begging. 'I saw him with these eyes – I was fourteen at the time – going about the street in a cowl with a sack on his back like a donkey. He was so worn by fasting and vigil and self-denial that he looked like an image of death, mere skin and bone, and in fact he died soon after. No one could look upon him without feeling ashamed of his own life.' Luther knew why he had turned his back on ease and luxury for such a life. Monasticism was the way to heaven. At the Last Judgment he would reap his reward; he would be treated, by virtue of his cowl, more favourably than the mass of sinners.

An altar-piece in one of the many churches depicted in symbolic form the teachings of the church, which was represented by a great ship in which 'there was not one layman not even a king or a prince. Alone in the prow with the Holy Ghost hovering above them were the Pope, the cardinals and the bishops, while at the oars along the sides of the ships were the priests and monks. So they went sailing on towards heaven. As for the laymen they were swimming in the water round the ship; some were drowning; some were holding on to the ropes thrown by the monks (who out of pity made over to them their own good works) and were hoping this way to stay with the ship and so make heaven of it with the others. Not a cardinal, or bishop, or monk or priest was in the water – only laymen!'

Gifted children are given to wondering about fundamental issues of life and death and Martin was no exception. He lived in a society in which there were reminders of death (and, worse, what awaited after death) at every turn. The whole fabric of the church was designed to deal with its inevitability but the tragedy was that religion had no message of hope being, as it was, largely an outward keeping of rules – a matter of fastings, penance, pilgrimages, processions, viewing of relics and so on. Perhaps that was all right as long as one did not think too much about it. Martin did think and his sensitive, probing conscience never let him feel that he had fulfilled the conditions.

The next school he attended was at Eisenach where some of his mother's relations lived. They might have been expected to befriend him but in the event it seems they did little for him. A story is told of one of the teachers there, Trebonius. On entering the classroom each morning he was in the habit of baring his head in the presence of so many future burgomasters, chancellors, doctors and consuls.

There Martin got to know the well-to-do and cultured family of Conrad and Ursula Cotta. The mother attended the same church as he did and her eye was often drawn to the lad with the sweet, ringing voice and serious expression. She showed him many kindnesses and eventually received him into their large, bright house in St George's Square. In their refined and happy home his personality blossomed. His love of music found full scope in the family sing-songs when he would accompany himself on the lute. Their kindness in opening their home to him and the many examples he saw of practical love and help to the under-privileged may have lain the foundation of his own legendary generosity in the years ahead. Recalling Mrs. Cotta in later years he said, 'There is nothing sweeter on earth than the heart of a good and pious woman.' No wonder he loved Eisenach – 'my own dear Eisenach' he called it. He was there for over three years.

In 1501 at the age of seventeen, he went to the University of Erfurt where he proved a brilliant student. It was in the library there that he first came across the Bible. 'I was twenty years of age before I ever saw the Bible and I had no idea that there existed any other gospels or epistles than those in the church service.' Opening it at the story of Samuel he was immediately entranced and often returned to the library to pore over its pages.

He revelled in study and in all the concomitants of student life. Round him he gathered a band of friends and many a jolly evening they had together, talking endlessly as students do, joking, singing and playing their musical instruments. Beneath his exuberance however there was an undercurrent of sadness and gloom, amounting almost to depression. There was a conflict in his mind.

He graduated Bachelor of Arts in 1503 and then in 1505 he gained his Master of Arts degree, much to the delight of his father who, when his son came home, showed his pride in him by henceforth addressing him with the respectful *Ihr* (you) rather than the more familiar *du* as used in the family. Hans and Margaret were seeing the fruits of the long years of self-denial and thrift. Martin, the pride of the family, must go on to study law for that was the route to the highest positions in the State. Hans even had one or two good marriage connections in mind. The prospect was bright. Martin would make a name for himself.

*****

It was a suffocatingly hot day as the young man neared Stotternheim on his way back to Erfurt. The weather matched his spirits – sunny and bright but oppressed by looming clouds that threatened change. Then the storm burst. A flash of lightning brought him to the ground. Thunder cracked open the skies, as if the heavens were clattering down on him. His life was over! 'St. Anne, help me!', he called out. 'I will become a monk!'

The storm passed and with it Martin's terror – but he could not shake off the recollection of that vow, wrung out of him when 'walled in by the terror and anguish of death' and immediately regretted. But he felt its compulsion. His mind made up, he acted. On reaching Erfurt he lost no time in inviting his friends to what proved to be a farewell party. Not till it was in full swing did he tell them that on the next day he was to enter the cloister.

Next morning he presented himself at the door of the Augustinian Monastery in Erfurt. Only then did he write to tell his father that he had become a monk.

What lay behind this apparently sudden decision and the vow forced from him almost apart from his will on that sultry second day of July? Saint Anne, the miners' saint, was familiar to him from babyhood. Many a time he must have heard her help invoked. But why 'I will become a monk'?

The short answer is that he was concerned about his standing before God. His intermittent and underlying moods of melancholy provide a clue. He said on one occasion that it was the harsh regime under which he had been brought up that drove him into *mönkerei* (monkishness) – not the monastery as such but the mental and emotional set that led in the end to the cloister. He found he could not live up to what he knew. At home strict obedience had been enjoined. At school he had learned the Ten Commandments and been well instructed in the ceremonies of the church. It would be surprising if a youth of his sensitivity and intelligence should not see that the commandments extended to thoughts and motives as well as to actions. It was not only that it was impossible to keep them – it was even impossible to know whether you had atoned sufficiently for even the smallest transgression.

Luther was acutely aware of his sinnership, not because his behaviour was worse than that of his contemporaries – there is nothing to indicate that – but because he was aware of how far short he fell in whatever he attempted. An illness and the death of a friend helped to focus his thoughts. What if he should die? He was not fit for heaven. The only way to save his soul, as everyone knew, was to enter holy orders. That he did not want to do. If only there could be some other way! Yet he could not simply put these worrying thoughts of death and judgment away. So he could not be wholly happy outside the cloister, nor could he think of life within it with pleasure. What about his father's reaction? His anger? His deep hurt and disappointment? His own reluctance and his father's anticipated disapproval tugged against his conscience. The pressure was insistent. So when the heavens thundered – and it might be his last warning – the fight went out of him.

His father was furious. A monk! And without telling him! Hans had no high opinion of monks. It was not just that they had no status. The lives of too many were blatantly immoral. Besides, Martin was not suited to the life. He wrote an angry letter. If Martin persisted in his monumental disobedience he could consider himself no longer part of the family. And for good measure there were no *Ihr*'s! 'My father nearly went mad about it.' Not long afterwards two of Martin's brothers died of the plague and friends suggested to the distraught father that perhaps he ought to devote his dearest son to God also. So Hans consented – reluctantly and with sorrow of heart. Martin knew that deep down 'he didn't really mean it.'

2

EXEMPLARY MONK

So on the 17th day of July, 1505, Luther became a monk and if salvation was to be had by keeping to the rules of the order he would bend all his energies to that end. He searched out and exploited to the full every iota of help that monasticism offered. The quiet round of prayers, fastings, vigils, meditations and chantings soothed his spirit and he seemed to have found the way of peace. Into this state of complacency he might have settled down as many monks did – a dangerous state from which too many had fallen into lives of immorality and cynical profligacy.

In May, 1507, the great day came when he was to celebrate his first mass. This was somewhat of an occasion at which the family were normally expected to be present. Hans Luther rode in with twenty friends from Mansfeld and made a handsome donation to the monastery. Martin took his place before the altar and began to recite the set introduction to the mass. Let him tell us what happened as he came to the words, 'We offer unto thee, the living, the true, the eternal God ...'

'At these words I was utterly stupefied and terror-stricken. I thought to myself, "How shall I address such Majesty, seeing that all men tremble in the presence of even an earthly prince? Who am I that I should lift up mine eyes or raise my hands to the divine Majesty? The angels surround him. At his nod the earth trembles. And shall I, a miserable little pygmy say, 'I want this, I ask for that'? For I am but dust and ashes and full of sin and I am speaking to the one living, eternal and true God."'

All his terror returned and only by a supreme effort was he able to continue. Before the great and unapproachable God he was puny and insignificant, and utterly sinful.

At the meal that followed Martin sought his father's reassurance that he really was reconciled to his becoming a monk. They had not met since that final visit home before Martin entered the monastery. Turning to the older man he asked,

'Dear father, why were you so set against my becoming a monk – and so angry? And perhaps even now you are not too pleased to see me here, although it is such a quiet and godly life, so full of peace?'

He should have left well alone! Hans' smothered resentment flared up.

'You learned scholars, have you not read in the Scriptures that you should honour your father and your mother? And here you have left me and your dear mother to fend for ourselves in our old age.'

'But father, I can do you more good by my prayers than if I had stayed in the world.'

He went on to tell how he had been called by God on the road to Stotternheim.

'God grant that it was not an apparition of the devil!' was Hans' rejoinder.

There was the rub. How did one know? Had he been misled by the devil disguised as an angel of light? Much later he wrote: 'Those words made a deep impression on me, as though they had been the words of God uttered by your lips. However firmly I closed my mind against them yet in my heart of hearts I have never been able to forget them. And yet I persevered in my own righteousness and despised you as being only a man. But you were right – God's commandment must take precedence. I should have suffered a thousand deaths rather than have acted as I did. No vow could ever merit such deception.'

Once again he was in turmoil, lost and defenceless before the high and holy One. His religious exercises no longer stilled his conscience. 'I was a good monk and followed the rules of my order so strictly that I can say if ever a monk got to heaven by his good works it was I. All my fellow-monks who knew me would bear me out. If I had kept on any longer I should have killed myself with vigils, prayers, reading and other exercises.'

The suspicion that perhaps these were mere human palliatives and not God-given, he tried to suppress as a temptation from the devil. But he could not hide from himself the plain fact that they could not deal with his sin.

'I went every day to confession but it was of no use to me. Still weighed down with sorrow, I was tormented by my crowding thoughts. Look, I cried, you are still full of envy, impatience and anger. It has not helped you one bit, oh wretched man, to have entered this sacred order.'

Now as haggard and worn as the mendicant friar he had seen in Eisenach, Luther was on the verge of a nervous breakdown. He was *the* monk *par excellence* and yet he was in despair.

Part of the trouble was that Luther craved assurance of salvation while the whole penitential system militated against it. To be forgiven he must confess his sins, so he did – for hours on end, ransacking his memory and wearying his confessors. But were there still some he had forgotten, some he did not recognise as sins, some he was hiding from himself (for 'the heart of man is deceitful ... who can know it?') If so, being unconfessed, they could not be forgiven. Moreover, while the church was concerned with the enumeration of particular sins, he came to feel more and more that these sins were a symptom of something deeper – the sinfulness of the person. The fruit was bad because the tree was bad. As for sins confessed, absolution was given if he was contrite – but was he contrite enough? How could anyone know?

Doubts about the efficacy of the sacraments were as nothing beside the doubts that assailed him about God himself. In common with his contemporaries he had imbibed a view of God as absolutely unconditioned, a law to himself. This made him seem capricious and his actions arbitrary. Even if satisfaction for sin were made he might not accept it. He, the Judge, was under no obligation to show mercy. He could choose not to in any particular case. Even worse were Luther's difficulties with his understanding of the doctrine of election.

'Is it not against all natural reason that God out of his mere whim deserts men, hardens them, damns them as if he delighted in sins and in such torments of the wretched for eternity, he who is said to be of such mercy and goodness? This appears iniquitous, cruel and intolerable in God, by which very many have been offended in all ages. And who would not be? I was myself more than once driven to the very abyss of despair so that I wished I had never been created. Love God? I hated him!' He might hate him, but he could not leave him alone.

There were ups and downs in his experience during these years though the prevailing mood was one of desperation. He spent all available time studying for his doctorate in theology and engaged wholeheartedly in the duties assigned him.

In 1510 he was chosen to go with another monk on a mission to Rome. Stories abound about that visit. Luther's interest there was not in the glories of ancient Rome far less those of Renaissance Italy but in the benefits to be gained by visiting the holy places to obtain spiritual advantages for himself or others. This was possible because of the 'treasury of merit' accumulated partly by the Lord Jesus Christ and partly by the saints who had produced more than enough righteousness for themselves. These superfluous merits were available for others and could be procured by the performance of good works. By good works was meant not deeds of moral worth but religious observances such as viewing of relics, pilgrimages, visits to shrines and vigils.

The moral degradation he saw in the Eternal City was a scandal but more disturbing were the thoughts beginning to form in his mind as he hurried from shrine to basilica to catacombs and then to Pilate's Staircase. As he climbed the Sancta Scala on hands and knees, repeating a Paternoster on each step in the conviction that each prayer would free a soul from Purgatory, he almost wished that his father and mother were dead that he might release them. (Well, at least his grandfather would benefit.) But, as he reached the top the thought intruded, 'Who knows whether it really is so?' Doubt again – this time as to whether the merits of the saints could be transferred. If not, that was another ray of hope gone.

That visit was decisive in one respect. It paved the way for Luther's coming break from the Roman Catholic Church. Much later he said, 'I would not have missed seeing Rome for a hundred thousand florins, for I might then have been afraid that I had done injustice to the Pope. But as we see, we speak.'

On his return to Erfurt he was transferred to the Augustinian Monastery in Wittenberg, which was to be his home for the rest of his life. At this time Wittenberg was a little walled town with a population of around three thousand – much smaller than Erfurt. Its whole length was less than one mile.

Small houses were huddled beside the river Elbe while a moat guarded the town on the other side. Down the two main streets flowed open water which worked the mill. At one end of the town was the monastery and at the other the Castle Church while the parish church, St Mary's, dominated the town square. And, of course, there was the University, founded in 1502 by the Elector of Saxony, Frederick the Wise, whose pride it was. Keen to enhance its status he was eager to attract some of the best minds of Germany as professors. So it was that Luther in 1511 was appointed to teach there.

He renewed acquaintance with the vicar-general of the Augustinian order, Johann von

Staupitz, and the two soon became firm friends. The older monk, a kind and perceptive man, noticed that this gifted and earnest young man who confessed his sins by the hour, was deeply distressed. He was not long in coming to understand him for he had himself been where Luther now stood. Wise and sympathetic, he did his best to direct his mind away from self-condemning introspection towards a more helpful line of thought. He had given him a Bible (the first Luther ever owned) with the words, 'Let the study of the Scriptures be your favourite occupation' which advice Luther gladly followed and indeed found helpful. On another occasion Staupitz told him, 'Christ does not terrify, he consoles.' Recalling them much later Luther comments, 'These words were a great relief to my mind and filled me with joy.' But after such respites he was again overtaken by despairing thoughts. It was as if he were blinkered, being able to see only the threatenings in the Scriptures.

Staupitz, appreciating his calibre, was almost at a loss as to how to help him – and found the solution in a bold administrative decision. As they sat together one day under the pear tree in the grounds of the cloister he informed him that he was to undertake preaching and become Professor of Bible at the University while studying for his doctor's degree. Luther was astounded. 'I had fifteen reasons against it and fifteen more when they were done,' he recalled. Staupitz wouldn't take no for an answer. Luther said he'd be killed with work. 'Fine,' said Staupitz. 'God has plenty of work for able men like you to do in heaven.'

So it came about that while teaching others Luther taught himself.

'I did not learn my divinity at once,' he recorded, 'but was constrained by my temptations to search deeper and deeper; for if one does not experience trials and temptations he cannot really understand the Holy Scriptures. St Paul had a devil that beat him with fists and with temptations drove him to study the Scriptures. Temptations hunted me into the Bible. God be praised I at length began to understand it.' Now as he lectured on the Psalms and Romans, the truth penetrated his own mind and emotions.

Here is his account of a moment of illumination. He was studying in the tower room.

'I greatly longed to understand Paul's Epistle to the Romans but always came to a standstill at that expression, "the righteousness of God" because I took it to mean that righteousness whereby God is just and deals justly in punishing the guilty. Now though I had been an exemplary monk, I felt myself to be a sinner before God, and was so troubled in conscience that I had no confidence that I could by any merit of my own ever assuage him. Therefore I did not love a just and angry God but rather hated him and complained against him. Night and day I pondered trying to make out the meaning of Paul. At last I saw the connection between the justice of God and the statement that "the just shall live by his faith". Then I understood that the justice of God is that righteousness by which God, quite freely and in sheer mercy, justifies us through faith. Thereupon I felt as if I had been reborn and had gone through open doors into Paradise. The whole of Scripture took on a new meaning and whereas I had formerly hated the expression "the righteousness of God" I now began to regard it as an inexpressibly sweet and comforting word so that this expression of Paul's became to me in very truth a gate to heaven.'

This new insight into the Scriptures transformed his total outlook – he had new views of God, Christ, the way of salvation, nature, art, marriage, the pleasures and trials of life, everything. It restored his personality to its true self, and not in the direction of more austerity but in the direction of freedom, of pleasure in all that is good and legitimate and of glad-hearted fun.

Now he understood that God was on the sinner's side. 'He who sees God as angry does not have the right view of him but sees only a curtain, as if a dark cloud hid his face.' Christ was no longer the awful Judge of the etchings, with lightnings coming out of his head, but the suffering Redeemer. 'The greatest wonder ever on earth is, that the Son of God died the shameful death of the cross. It is astonishing that the Father should say to his only Son, who by nature is God: "Go, let them hang you on the gallows." To us true Christians, it is the greatest comfort: for we therein recognise that the merciful Lord God and Father so loved the poor condemned world, that he did not spare his only begotten Son, but gave him up for us all, that whosoever believes in him should not perish, but have everlasting life.'

3

RELUCTANT REBEL

All the elements of Luther's mature theology were now present to his understanding, painfully worked out as they had been through his own experience. His prodigious programme of work continued to keep him busy. In October, 1516, he wrote, 'I would need two secretaries; I do almost nothing all day but write letters. I lecture in the cloister, read at meals, preach, direct the students' studies, supervise eleven monasteries, inspect the fish-ponds at Leitzkau, settle the quarrel at Torgau, expound St Paul and the Psalms and, as I said, see to my mail. Add to that the temptations of the world, the flesh and the devil. See how much spare time I have!'

As pastor of St Mary's parish church he preached to the townspeople and peasants from the surrounding countryside. His new message of hope found a ready hearing. All this purposeful activity took place, however, against a backdrop of growing uneasiness.

Up till this time he was an unknown monk in a small town 'on the edge of civilisation' as someone once described it. In 1517 he was catapulted into the centre of controversy quite without wish or intent on his part. It was over the issue of indulgences.

The sacrament of penance was one of the remedies for sin prescribed by the church. After confession accompanied by contrition the penitent had to do penance, that is, a punishment prescribed by the priest by which the sinner atoned in part for his sin. Part – or all – of this sentence could be remitted by purchase of an indulgence. By the end of the 16th century these indulgences could also be used to buy off years in Purgatory. They could be bought on behalf of friends or relatives already in that dread place.

The logic behind them was this. The church's treasury of merit was at the Pope's disposal. He could give of it to anyone he chose by means of a certificate of indulgence. The temptation to use them as money-spinners proved irresistible. St Peter's Church in Rome was being rebuilt and money was badly needed so there was a great drive to sell indulgences. The Pope's chief agent was Tetzel. This notorious salesman threw all circumspection to the winds.

Some of his sales talk has come down to us: 'There is no sin so great that an indulgence cannot remit.' 'Priest, noble, merchant, wife, youth, maiden! Do you not hear your parents and friends who are dead? They cry from the abyss, "We are suffering horrible torments.

A trifling sum would save us: you can give it; will you not save us?"' And of course the jingle:

'As soon as the coin in the coffer rings,
The soul from Purgatory springs',
or
'Drop a coin in the offertory,
And free a soul from Purgatory'.

A further scandal was the bargain struck with Albert of Brandenburg who by the age of twenty-three had become archbishop twice – at a price which had put him in debt to the wealthy Fugger family. An arrangement was made between the Pope and Fuggers, the bankers, that they should receive half of the sales from indulgences and an agent from the bank actually accompanied Tetzel to make sure the bargain was kept.

Luther was not alone in his misgivings which came to a head in November, 1517. The precipitating factor was an exhibition of relics to be held in Wittenberg. This collection of over five thousand items had been built up by the Elector Frederick over many years. He had travelled far and wide for his holy hoard which, according to a catalogue drawn up and illustrated by the artist Lucas Cranach in 1509, included one twig of Moses' burning bush, one tooth of St Jerome, from the manger in Bethlehem one straw, of Our Lady four hairs. They were to be available for viewing and those who took advantage of the offer could (for a fee) have indulgences for reduction of Purgatory for periods of up to thousands of years. During 1516 Luther in his preaching pointed out the futility of them. It was not to the concept of indulgences as such that he objected but to their abuse. For one thing they encouraged people to sin since they could buy off sin's penalty. On the other hand those who were really concerned about their sins were being cheated, and his pastor's heart could not bear it. He thought it was time that the whole question was thrashed out. So he drew up a number of propositions for debate, ninety-five in all (in Latin, of course, the language of theological discussion). Here are some:

> Every truly repentant Christian has a full remission of penalty and guilt even without indulgences.

> Christians are to be taught that he who sees his neighbour in want and does nothing to help, yet gives his money for indulgences, does not buy papal indulgences but God's wrath.

> If the Pope has the power of releasing anyone from Purgatory, why does he not, holy as he is, abolish Purgatory altogether by letting everyone out? This would be a far more worthy use of his power than freeing souls for money. And for what, moreover? A building!'

As was current practice when drawing attention to a matter for debate he would pin them on the church door, thus drawing the attention of the members of the faculty to them – and little dreaming of the furore that would follow.

4

CATHERINE

Long before dawn on All Saint's Day, 1517, a monk made his way across Wittenberg to the Castle Church and nailed a placard on the great wooden doors. The hammerblows reverberated throughout Europe and changed the course of history. They reached into a convent of the Cistercian order in Nimptsch and there set in motion events that would profoundly affect Luther's own life.

Nimptsch was a small town six miles to the south of Grimma, and about twenty miles south east of Leipzig. The convent was exclusively for ladies of high birth. It was not as strict as some later orders; the nuns were not forbidden to speak and news from the outside world trickled in – and was doubtless much discussed as they bent over their embroidery or distilled herbs.

One of them, Catherine von Bora, was eighteen when Luther burst into the world with his ninety-five theses. Little is known of her childhood. She was born on 29th January, 1499, to an aristocratic family who had fallen on hard times. Bora is a Slavonic name. The family seat was at Stein-laussig, near Bitterfeld in the district of Meissen. There were at least three brothers in the family though by this time only one, Hans, was living . It is thought that her mother died when Catherine was a baby and that when her father remarried she was sent to a Benedictine convent at Brehna. She was then three years old.

At the age of ten she was transferred to the convent of Marienthron in Nimptsch, where she learned to read and write and acquired some knowledge of Latin. She also became proficient in needlework and learned how to distil herbs. In such activities punctuated by vigils, sacraments, choir-singing and processions the nuns passed their days. It would be strange if some did not find the confinement and monotony irksome, especially those who were not there by choice. Catherine had taken the veil at the age of sixteen but with how much alacrity is not known. Some were nuns for purely family reasons – perhaps to swell the dowry of a sister. There were, however, those who had a vocation, for whom the convent was the only way they knew to heaven and no doubt they would try to squeeze as much meaning as possible from the round of religious observances. Among Catherine's companions were Veronica and Margaret von Zeschau, Eva and Margaret von Schönfeld and Magdalene von Staupitz whose uncle was Dr Luther's friend. Catherine's aunt Magdalene was also in the convent.

In 1516 Dr. Luther visited the monastery in nearby Grimma and it is likely that news of his teachings reached the nuns. He preached to the ordinary people in German! He said that God was merciful, and dependable. You did not need to approach him via St Anne or St Elizabeth or any of the hundred and one saints in the heavenly hierarchy but through Jesus Christ. And salvation was to be had by faith – good works could not earn it. If that were so ... then salvation was obtainable in the outside world? Not exclusively in convents?

Then came 1st November, 1517, and the ninety-five theses. The document was translated into German, rushed to the printers and read everywhere. What a commotion! A lone monk had challenged the Pope. Someone was asserting boldly what many had been muttering, for there were some astute folk who grudged paying good German gulden to finance a building in Rome. Implicit in the theses was a questioning of the whole system taught by the church as the way of salvation, and there were some who sensed that there was more in them than met the eye.

One event followed the other and some news probably penetrated the convent – the attack by Tetzel; rumours that Luther was to be burnt at the stake, that the Pope had summoned him to Rome, that the Elector was demanding a fair trial; the demand from Cajetan, 'Luther must recant.'

In 1519 Luther was again in Grimma and in the following year his writings were causing a stir, and no wonder. God could be served as well outside the convent as in! God had ordained marriage, so priests should be free to marry! What was more, he proved that these ideas were not his own but were derived from the Scriptures. And he insisted that it is the Scriptures that must decide all these questions – not Popes or cardinals. Then, Luther is excommunicated – the ultimate sanction one might think. Followed by the mandate to burn his books – the best advertisement one might say. Yet he was the people's hero. They were saying, 'Nine tenths are for Luther and one tenth against the Pope.' In Mainz when the executioner asked, before applying the torch, 'Have these books been legally condemned?', the crowd roared, 'No!' and the books were saved. In Erfurt a crowd of rollicking students threw all the copies of the papal bull of excommunication into the river yelling, 'Let's see if the "bulloons" will float!' At a bonfire elsewhere one of the crowd taunted the friar who was supervising it, 'You would see better if the ashes of Luther's books got in your eyes!'

Another bonfire – this time in Wittenberg. The students piled on books of scholastic theology and canon law and the dancing flames lit up the Elster Gate. Luther stepped forward and into the pyre dropped the papal bull.

In April, 1521, he entered Worms to stand before the Emperor, nobles and church dignitaries – one lone monk against 'all the world'. He was asked,

'Do you or do you not repudiate your books? Give me a plain answer without horns.'

His reply thrilled Europe:

'Since your Majesty desires a clear answer I will give you one without horns and without teeth. Unless I am convinced by Scripture and plain reason, for my conscience is captive to the Word of God, I cannot and I will not recant for it is neither right nor safe for a Christian to go against his conscience. Here I stand. I cannot do otherwise. God help me. Amen.'

He was outlawed. Suddenly he disappeared. For months no word was heard about him. Was he alive? He was – for in the September of the following year his first translation of the New Testament in German was being circulated. Did one enter the convent at Nimptsch? The next news was that the professor was back at his post in Wittenberg.

Luther's writings were finding their way into cloisters where they were eagerly discussed. The very foundations of the ecclesiastical system were being probed and tested. Monks were leaving and even setting up homes of their own. There was an exodus from the Franciscan Monastery of the Holy Cross in Grimma. This must have given rise to much talk in the Nimptschen convent as the nuns bent over their endless embroidery. They, no less than the people of Germany at large, were either exhilarated or dismayed by all that had happened since 1517. All might seem as calm, even monotonous, as usual but beneath the surface there was a ferment of suppressed excitement and frustration.

These world-shaking events took place while Catherine was in her late teens and early twenties – an age given to deep questionings about the meaning of life and death. She and eleven others had become disenchanted with life in the cloister. It is not certain just how much they knew or understood of the new teaching (perhaps a great deal) but gradually one found courage to tell another of the longing to get out into the world again and by the end of 1522 there was a little band of twelve, among them the Zeschau and Schönfeld sisters and Magdalene von Staupitz who was older than the others. They decided to do the unthinkable and write to their people asking them to have them home again.

The replies came – No in each case; some kindly (it was all right for monks to leave, they could make their way in the world), some harsh (how could they think of bringing such disgrace on their families?). If their secret was out and they were punished, they no doubt did their penance but were not repentant. They were at a standstill however and, one can imagine, disheartened. Except Magdalene von Staupitz, who was possibly in touch with her uncle. At her suggestion they appealed to Luther to help them in their predicament and he did come to their aid – by delegating. He got in touch with his good friend, the merchant Leonhard Koppe, a respected citizen of Torgau, asking him to do what he could. Koppe went from time to time to Nimptsch, some sixty miles away, to deliver barrels of herring to the convent. Somehow he got word to the nuns to be ready to leave on the night of the 4th April. He would be waiting for them. It was a dangerous undertaking for the penalty for abducting nuns was death. Moreover, though both Nimptsch and Torgau were in Saxony the road they were to take led through the territory of Duke George, one of Luther's most inveterate enemies, who would be only too glad to make a scandal of the enterprise.

So, on the Eve of the Resurrection, all twelve made the venture and escaped undetected from Catherine's window on the south wall. Koppe and two others – his nephew and a friend, Wolfgang Tommitsch, helped them over the boundary wall into his covered wagon. Crouched among the herring barrels they held their breath (and surely the drivers did too) as the load of casks bumped over the cobbled roadway and on into the dark countryside. The story goes that they were challenged on the way across Duke George's land but managed to hoodwink their questioners and next day they arrived in Torgau. They'd pulled it off and doubtless after the first flush of exhilaration they wondered, 'What now?'

5

THE PEASANTS' WAR

Leonhard Koppe, honest merchant and one-time city accountant of Torgau, trundled on the 7th April, 1523, into Wittenberg with a delivery for Herr Doktor Luther. A student gleefully reported, 'A wagon load of vestal virgins has just come to town, all more eager for marriage than for life. God grant them husbands lest worse befall.' Luther, in recognition of his friends' resourcefulness and courage, later publicly presented him with a written address.

The escapade caused a sensation. Three of the girls had been received by their families. In a letter of 8th April to his friend Link, Luther wrote, 'Yesterday I received from their prison nine nuns belonging to the Nimptschen convent, among whom were the two Zeschaus and Magdalene Staupitz.' To the court preacher, Spalatin, he wrote, 'But you will ask what I intend to do with them. First, I will inform their parents and beg them to receive them into their homes again. If they refuse then I shall see that they are otherwise provided for. I already have promises of help for some and I shall get the rest married if I can. Their escape is quite wonderful. Please exercise your charity by begging, in my name, some money from your rich courtiers so that they can be looked after for one or two weeks till I can get them settled.'

Catherine von Bora was placed with the town-clerk of Wittenberg, Philip Reichenbach, and his wife Elsa. A childless couple, they made her welcome and there she found a happy home where she presumably acquired the housewifely skills that were later to stand her in such good stead. The freedom and variety of life in a comfortable home must have appealed to her greatly while the practical side of her nature found an outlet in gardening and housework.

Through Dr Luther she became friendly with one of his theological students, Hieronymous Baumgärtner, who belonged to one of the noble families of Nürnberg. It would appear there was an understanding between them but when he returned to his home he seemed to lose interest. Possibly his family objected. In a letter of 24th October, 1524, in which he asked a favour of him, Luther wrote, 'Moreover, if you intend marrying Catherine von Bora, do make haste before she is given to someone else, for C. Glatz, pastor in Orlamunde, is ready waiting. She has not yet got over her love for you. I wish you two were married. Farewell.'

Well, he married someone else. In the years to come he gained distinction and became a close friend of Luther and Melancthon.

Places were found for the other eight and in time suitable marriages were arranged for some of them. Why didn't Luther marry one himself, someone suggested. Luther's reply, in a letter of 30th November, 1524, was that he had no such intention; it wasn't that he was a stone lacking the normal feelings of a man, or that he had anything against marriage, but there was no point since he expected any day to be put to death as a heretic. However, he was in the hands of God who could change his heart and change it again ...

By this time he had other things on his mind. Since October there had been unrest among the peasants. Ground down by feudal service and given, in such of Luther's writings as *The Freedom of the Christian*, a glimpse of the dignity of the individual they drew up a manifesto *The Twelve Articles* in which they set out their programme for land reform and social justice. It was reasonable and conservative in tone: they sought to subject themselves to Scripture; only if any demand were proved not agreeable to Scripture would they give it up, 'seeing that Christ has redeemed and bought us all with the precious shedding of his blood, the lowly as well as the grand.' There was no attack on government. 'The gospel is not a cause of rebellion and disturbance.' The Lutheran undertones are unmistakable. They sent him a copy. To whom besides should they turn?

Hadn't he said that in Christendom 'all things are in common and each man's goods are the other's, and nothing is simply a man's own'? He criticised several aspects of it but undertook to do what he could – short of armed rebellion. He would not intrude on the sphere of the magistrate. That would be to forsake his calling as a minister. Besides, he had long ago made it clear that he would on no account support the taking of arms by the private citizen. That way lay chaos, murder and bloodshed. Scripture says, 'The powers that be are ordained of God', and Luther concluded that 'no insurrection is ever right no matter what the cause.'

Representing the peasants before the princes he (as a good advocate) spoke more favourably of their claims than he had when replying to them. They were fair and just; each side should listen to the other and take the matter to disinterested arbitrators. His powerful appeal went unheeded.

Denied their rights the peasants went on the rampage, pillaging and burning castles and cloisters in uncoordinated and uncontrolled mass madness. Much of their activity was at the level of plundering wine cellars and depleting fish ponds. Starting in the Black Forest the rebellion spread like wildfire. Twice Luther intervened to plead for moderation but in vain. Appalled at this result of his written rhetoric he dashed off a pamphlet, *Against the Robbing and Murdering Hordes of Peasants* in which he called for the actual insurgents (not the peasants as a whole) to be put down with the sword, and quickly, for this was the best hope of containing the conflagration. He said, 'If the peasant is in open rebellion, then he is outside the law of God, for rebellion is not simply murder, but it is like a great fire which attacks and lays waste a whole land.'

The nobles had no need of such advice; they were already butchering without discrimination and their excesses sickened him next. He wrote another tract pleading this time for mercy to be shown to the peasants but it had no effect. On the 15th May at the Battle of Frankenhausen one hundred thousand peasants were slaughtered and by June the rebellion was broken.

The war had claimed one hundred and thirty thousand peasants in all. Luther called now for mercy to the guilty as well as the innocent, but no-one was inclined to listen. He was being maligned on all sides.

The peasants felt he had betrayed them while the Roman Catholic princes blamed him for starting it all. To his own spirit it dealt a lasting blow. It shook his trust in the common man and affected his judgment when engaged in the politics of church government.

By this time he was almost alone in the monastery for the monks had all left. In the autumn of 1524 he had given up wearing the cowl. He was no longer a monk.

The business of the nuns was not finished yet. His correspondence is peppered with references to his attempts to marry them off. And some of his friends were urging him again - wasn't it time he was getting married himself since he was so good at advocating it for others? In reply to some such suggestion from Spalatin he wrote in April, 'If you want my example here it is: I have had three wives at once and have loved them so well that I have lost two of them to other husbands. The third I am managing to hold on to with my left hand and she is perhaps about to be snatched away from me. It's you who are really the timid lover who do not dare to marry even one.'

The last one was Catherine who was still in domestic service with the Reichenbachs. Luther tried to get her interested in Dr Glatz but she would have none of him. Already at twenty-five rather old (for those days) to be still unmarried she doubtless felt her position keenly but she knew her own mind and Glatz was not for her. (He is said to have later proved himself unworthy of his calling, so did she have good discernment?) When Luther's friend, Amsdorf, visited Wittenberg late in March or early in April she asked him to let Luther know that she would on no account consider Glatz. 'I'd rather have Dr Luther himself,' she added, 'or you!' There are some intriguing questions. Did she mean it or was she joking, taking it for granted that they were both rather old for marrying and therefore out of the question? (But then, she actually did not consider Luther too old – as events were to prove.) If she meant or half-meant it, does it show a mild attachment to both, or a cold dispassionate judgment that they were both eminent and suitable potential husbands? Or, as seems more likely, did this strong-minded girl know not only whom she did not want to marry, but also whom she did? Luther, as well as likeable personal qualities, had the glamour of being famous and the two had had every opportunity of getting to know each other well as Luther often visited the Reichenbach home.

Whatever the import of the remark, Amsdorf repeated it to Luther and he remembered it long enough to repeat it to his father when he visited his home shortly after this.

6

WEDDING BELLS

Everybody's hand was against Luther. In June he wrote, 'Now lords, priests, peasants are all against me and threaten me with death.' Then, as if to put the finishing touch and bring added opprobrium down on himself, what should he do but get married! And just as suddenly and apparently out of the blue as with the other big decisions of his life. To Link he wrote, 'Suddenly, and while I was occupied with far other thoughts, the Lord has plunged me into marriage.' But as with those other decisions the suddenness was more apparent than real. That he had been toying (however tentatively and negatively) with the idea of marriage is evident from his correspondence. When, as far back as 1520, he had written that priests must be free to marry and had approved of Carlstadt's marriage – 'I am very pleased. I know the girl' – he was yet of the opinion that it was a different matter with monks since they were under vows. He was taken aback at Carlstadt's contention that monks should also be free to marry. 'Will our Wittenbergers give wives to monks? They won't give me one!' he wrote from the Wartburg in 1521. But monks were already leaving the monastery and marrying. Melancthon wondered what Luther thought about it. Should they be urged to go back? 'The real question is not whether vows can be kept, but whether they have been enjoined by God,' said Luther.

He searched the Scriptures and the outcome was the booklet, *On Monastic Vows* in which he said that such vows are contrary to the Bible's teaching and Christian liberty. The monastic life is not superior to other callings. At a stroke this concept raised the status of all work. Every kind of work may equally be a vocation. The home is as sacred as the monk's cell. The mother at the bedside of a sick child is doing God's work every bit as much as a nun keeping vigil in the convent. Since such vows are contrary to Scripture they are not binding, he concluded. The booklet he dedicated to his 'dearest father' no doubt giving the old man cause for hope ...

To please his father was one of the reasons he gave for getting married. On a visit home in late April, in the course perhaps of bringing him up to date on the business of the nuns he mentioned Catherine's remark to Amsdorf. Hans welcomed the idea. Why not? He would dearly love Martin to marry and continue the family name. Was Luther already thinking that way himself, merely sounding his father out?

Friends kept up the barrage of advice. If marriage was a fine thing why didn't he take a wife? He needed one in that big monastery with only himself and the prior managing as best they could. Besides, example is better than precept. His enemies had their say too. 'Should this monk marry, the whole world and even the devil, would roar with laughter and he himself will destroy what he has built up.'

One snag was that he was expecting martyrdom at any moment. However, this paradoxically, pushed him in the direction of matrimony. On 1st July, 1523, the first martyrs of the Reformation, Henry Voes and John Esch, were burnt at the stake in Brussels. These two young Augustinian monks had been educated at Wittenberg and Luther wrote a hymn in their honour. They were the first of many. If Luther himself were to die soon he must marry so that his example would help to safeguard his teaching.

To Spalatin on the 10th April he wrote, 'I find so many reasons for urging others to marry, that I shall soon be brought to it myself notwithstanding that enemies never cease to condemn the married state.' A few days later, before setting out for Eisleben and home, he wrote again to Spalatin (who had been averse to marriage but was now intending to get married) saying that he might well be beaten to it. In a letter of 4th May to Chancellor Rühel, his brother-in-law, appears the first mention of

Catherine. In spite of the devil he would 'take my Katie in marriage before I die. I hope they will not take from me my courage and my joy.' He would at once give her a status and vindicate his views. In early June he said, 'I believe in marriage, and I intend to get married before I die, even though it should be only a betrothal like Joseph's.'

The moment of decision would seem to have crept up on him half unawares but, typically, having made up his mind he acted. Asked about this time what he thought of long engagements, 'Don't procrastinate,' he said. 'The gifts of God are to be taken on the wing.' How he and Katie came to an agreement is not known. Luther believed that such matters were between the two concerned and God, and he was not telling. He was not in love with Katie or so he thought. In a letter to Spalatin he wrote, 'If I had seriously thought of marrying before, I should have chosen Eva von Schönfeld, but she has married a young student.' She was one of the nine, and he became a royal physician. It was a happy marriage. Speaking twelve years later he said, 'At that time I was not in love with my Katie at all, but God wanted me to take pity on the forsaken one.'

On Tuesday, 13th June, they were publicly betrothed in the home of the Reichenbachs. The only friends present were Dr Apel, Justus Jonas, Lucas Cranach and his wife, and Dr Bugenhagen who performed the ceremony. This was the real marriage ceremony; in the eyes of the law they were now man and wife. He was forty-one, she was twenty-six.

The public ceremony which was arranged for the 27th was really a big wedding party after which the bride was conducted to her new home. Letters of invitation were sent out.

To Spalatin: 'You must come to my wedding. I have made the angels laugh and the devils weep.'

To brave Leonhard Koppe (of course!): 'I am going to get married. God likes to work miracles and to make a fool of the world. You must come to the wedding.'

To another: 'No doubt the rumour of my marriage has reached you. I can hardly believe it myself but the witnesses are too strong to gainsay. The wedding will be next Tuesday in the presence of my father and mother. I hope you can bring some venison and come yourself.'

To Chancellor Rühel: 'According to the wish of my dear father, I have taken to myself a wife; and so as to quash rumour and remonstrance I have lost no time in getting it settled. In the present state of unrest and danger, I cannot press you to come; but if you would like to and can manage it, and can bring with you my dear father and mother it would give me great joy.'

The great day arrived. The citizens of Wittenberg were in gay mood as they came out to congratulate their own dear Doktor. At ten o'clock, as the bells rang out, Luther led Katie from her home to the parish church. There, before the great gate and in the presence of the crowd, the religious ceremony took place. The procession then made its way to the Augustinian cloister where a banquet was held. A dance in the town hall followed with another banquet in the evening bringing the festivities to a close. It had been a day to remember. To crown Luther's joy his mother and father were there and there was nothing to cloud their rejoicing.

Their home was the Augustinian monastery which Luther had entered fourteen years before as a young monk beginning his lectureship. It had been gifted to them by the Elector. The University presented them with a beautifully chased silver cup lined with gold. The city honoured them with a fine cellar of wine and beer (Wittenberg was a beer-brewing centre) as well as the customary year's supply of wine given to its newly-weds. Another gift was a double-linked ring, one with a diamond and the initials M.L.D., the other with a ruby and the letters Cv.B. Inscribed inside are the words, *Was Got zusamen fiegt* on the one and on the other *Sol kein Mensch scheiden* (What God has joined together, let no man put asunder). There is another ring, possibly from Catherine to Luther, inscribed, 'D. Martino Luthero Catharina v. Boren 13 Jun. 1525'.

As Luther had expected, though many of his friends were delighted that he was married, there were many critics. Even some of his friends had reservations, feeling that somehow or other he had lowered himself. Melancthon at first disapproved, as Luther had thought he might and for that reason had not invited him to the betrothal on the 13th though he did ask him to the reception on the 27th. It says much for the impact that this one decision of his made, that centuries later attacks were still being made on it. Among contemporaries Erasmus had some rather scandalous things to say for which he later apologised. And Henry VIII of England (of all people!) called him 'a mangy dog', 'the Hell-wolf', two of the milder expressions in a vituperative letter.

That they were happy together there can be no doubt, and mutually beneficial. He thanked God for a 'pious and faithful wife' to whom he could safely trust his heart. His 'dear rib' was 'gentle, obedient and kind in all things far beyond my hopes. I would not exchange my poverty with her, for all the riches of Croesus without her.' Again he said, 'I would not part from my Katie, no not to gain all France and Venice.' Late in life he said, 'Next to God's Word, his best gift is a pious, cheerful, God-fearing, home-keeping wife with whom you can live in peace and tranquillity; to whom you can entrust your goods and body and life' and, to let her know it was not all one way, 'Katie, you have a pious husband who loves you; you are a very empress; thanks be to God.'

Their home became a pattern of mutual love and esteem which paved the way for romanticism in marriage, something rare in the Germany of that time where the view of marriage was still largely that of the Middle Ages in which the main considerations were preserving the family name and securing property. This was Luther's own view though a letter he wrote interceding for a student shows that he considered the whole question was one for mutual understanding and toleration.

> 'I have already written you concerning your son John who has fallen in love with a very nice girl but since there has been no reply I feel I must write again. Since he is so much in love with the girl who, as well as being quiet and gentle, is quite his equal socially, I think you could be satisfied that by humbly seeking your consent he has shown the obedience a son should; now you, on your part, may show the love of a mother by giving your consent. For although we have written that children should not become engaged without their parents' consent, parents should not on the other hand keep their children from marrying those whom they love. They must both give way. So, please, act like a mother and help him out of his martyrdom ...'

Together, and without in the least intending it, they created an open, trusting and caring partnership that left its stamp on German home life for centuries to come. Luther's views on marriage developed with his experience of it. His earlier pronouncements, of course, must be read against the background of the prevailing veneration of the single state with a corresponding denigration of marriage and alongside that the irregularities and immorality that often (not always) attended a profession of celibacy. At first he advocated marriage for its basic physical benefits but after his wedding he came to lay more emphasis on the opportunity for character development that marriage afforded.

His views derive ultimately from Scripture as might be expected. The man is the head of the home where he is to rule in love. The wife is to love, honour and obey her husband for he is her head as God is his. Children are to honour and obey their parents while parents, on their part, are to see to it that they do not provoke their children to anger. There is no room for rampant individualism. Each must consider the other. The duties and responsibilities inherent in married life develop qualities that might not otherwise emerge. And the total context within which all this takes place is love. 'The first love is a kind of intoxication,' he said. 'When this had worn off then comes the real marriage love.'

Oh, there were trials and tribulations in marriage to be sure – bawling babies (the sort of thing that caused the Church fathers to give marriage a bad name), chattering wives and the struggle to make ends meet. 'My whole life is patience. I have to have patience with the Pope, heretics, my family, and Katie.' However, he had to admit it was good for him. Perhaps his working philosophy might be summed up in his advice to a newly-wed, 'Rather keep the little queen in a good humour than be always looking for just cause of anger against her. Still, you must not let yourself be treated any way!'

His view of the dignity of all callings meant that he regarded his wife's work as, in its sphere, equal in worth to his own. Thus she was able to engage her considerable business and administrative abilities to the full. He would have endorsed George Herbert's *The Elixir* written a century later.

Teach me my God and King
In all things thee to see,
And what I do in anything,
To do it as for thee.

All may of thee partake;
Nothing can be so mean,
Which with this tincture, 'for thy sake',
Will not grow bright and clean.

A servant with this clause
Makes drudgery divine:
Who sweeps a room as for thy laws
Makes that and the action fine.

This is the famous stone
That turneth all to gold:
For that which God doth touch and own
Cannot for less be told.

7

EARLY MARRIAGE

The Augustinian convent in which Luther and his bride made their home was a large three-storeyed building backing on the town wall. There were forty rooms on the ground floor alone. The steep roof was covered with red tiles. The back windows looked out over the Elbe while in front of the building was a large garden in which stood the pear tree under which Staupitz and Luther had sat talking many years before.

'There is a lot to get used to in the first year of marriage,' Luther discovered. 'You wake up in the morning and find a pair of pigtails on the pillow which were not there before.' The pigtails belonged to a determined young lady with a mind of her own. Luther had suspected her of being proud and perhaps he was right. Or it may simply be that a certain reserve and dignity made her appear aloof. At any rate she had a strong sense of her own identity and worth which she would need if she was not to feel swamped and overlooked in her husband's forceful presence. A shrinking violet would not have suited him anyway. His personality needed someone to come up against, someone who would always be herself. He called her 'my lord Katie' or on occasion pronounced her name Kette, German for 'chain'. He said that if he wanted an obedient wife he would have to carve one for himself out of stone.

In a portrait painted by Cranach about 1525 she looks out from calm, wide-set eyes under well-defined brows, the expression direct, almost appraising. The forehead is high and her dark hair is parted at the centre, with a 'widow's peak'. The cheeks are rather full and the mouth small with firm, shapely lips. It is not a particularly pretty face; rather it is strong and well-shaped. A contemporary remarked that a portrait of her as an older woman was remarkably like one of Luther's mother in her old age and a like similarity had been noted between Luther and his mother.

In the parallel portrait of Luther the brooding, thinking eyes rivet you. They seem to have been remarkable. Brown in colour they have been variously described as 'deep as a lake', 'sparkling like stars', 'terrible as lightning', for his expressive features reflected the play of his thoughts and emotions. The bone structure is strong with high wide cheekbones and a fine brow.

The first description of him by a contemporary records his appearance in 1519 at the debate in Leipzig. 'He is of medium height, in the vigour of manhood with a clear, penetrating voice. He is refined and friendly, in no way dour or arrogant; he is at ease in any company; he is vivacious, witty, always relaxed and cheerful no matter how hard pressed by his adversaries.'

At first they were very poor. Catherine's father, an ardent Catholic, had refused to have anything more to do with her after she left the convent so she brought no wealth with her. Luther's salary, even when doubled as it was now, was hardly equal to the demands made on it. In 1526 he bought a lathe as a means of supporting his family if need be but one doubts if he ever found the time to do much with it. Catherine set to to capitalise on what they had – ground. She got Luther interested in gardening and it became his delight, 'the recreation I most dearly love.' They grew cabbage, lettuce, peas, beans, radishes, melons, cucumbers and strawberries, perhaps more. At the end of letters on church polity come requests from Katie for cucumber and melon seeds from Nürnberg or perhaps radish seeds from Erfurt. In a letter to Elizabeth of Brunswick he writes, 'My dear Katie and I thank your Grace for the cheese. I am sending your Royal Highness some slips of mulberry and fig trees, the only rare things I have at present.'

They acquired an orchard outside the village, beyond the Elster gate, and there Katie grew apples, pears, grapes, peaches and nuts. Luther built a fountain and later a small summerhouse. There was a fishpond stocked with trout, carp, pike and perch. Katie also looked after hens, ducks, pigs and cows (and saw to the slaughtering of them!). In a letter to his friend Justus Jonas, written in October, 1535, he says: 'My lord Katie greets you. She rides, drives, plants our fields, buys our cattle and pastures them and over and above she has a bet of fifty gulden that she will read the whole Bible by Easter. She is hard at it and has begun the fifth book of Moses.'

Katie proved to be a capable housewife too. She was thrifty – some even said parsimonious but this is hardly fair as someone needed to keep the household affairs on an even keel. Luther did not worry about debts – when Katie paid one another was sure to turn up. If he had money he gave it to any in need. If he had no money he blithely gave away the first valuable to hand. On one occasion a student came to him bemoaning the fact that he could not pay his fare home and in spite of Katie's remonstrating eye upon him he handed over a silver cup – for they didn't need to drink from silver, did they? Characteristically she found her own way of dealing with his exasperating generosity. Once he wrote to a friend saying he was sending him a vase. Then follows a P.S., 'Katie's hidden it.'

In another matter she had less success. He would take no money for his writings (or, for that matter, for his preaching) though Katie pertinently pointed out that the only ones to benefit from that were the publishers whose fat pockets bulged with gulden she could put to good use.

She managed not only the household; she also managed Dr Luther very well. She always called him *Herr Doktor* and addressed him by the respectful *Ihr* rather than the familiar *du* (in public anyway). He was given to ills of various sorts some no doubt finding their origin in the stringencies of his monastic life. At different times he suffered from catarrh, kidney stones, constipation, insomnia, dizziness, and a buzzing – 'not a buzzing but a roll of thunder' – in his head and her knowledge of herbs was useful to him. Others benefited too. In a letter to Spalatin he wrote, 'Greet your dear wife. My Katie sends you these roots which you may not have. They are a very good remedy against the stone and have helped me and many others.'

This caring side of Katie comes out in another letter he wrote, this time to a young father. 'My Katie greets you and wishes you much happiness over the birth of your son; she strongly advises that all the milk that can be spared should be kept for the little one till he can take other food; also that your wife must be made to take very good care of herself. But as a husband, I'm sure you know all this already – though my Katie seems to have her doubts!'

Their home became a centre of open-hearted hospitality where friends, relatives, students, birds of passage, lords and ladies, and down-and-outs were made welcome. Katie was introduced to a warm-hearted circle of friends, working together towards a common end and knit together in love and trust.

Luther's closest friend, the brilliant and gentle Philip Melancthon, Professor of Greek in the University, was fourteen years younger than Luther. They lived near each other; in fact their back gardens adjoined and there was much coming and going between the families. Then there was Justus Jonas, ten years younger than Luther and the eloquent preacher in the Castle Church. The wives of these two were called Catherine and the three Catherines were very good friends. Bugenhagen was the pastor of the town church. Lucas Cranach, the portrait painter, and his wife were friends also. Spalatin, the preacher at the Elector's court, was the same age as Luther and the two had been fellow-students at Erfurt. He married not long after Luther and invited his friend to the wedding in November. Luther wrote:

'Gladly would I be at your wedding, to rejoice with them that do rejoice, but the tears and fears of my wife prevent me. She dreamt last night that murderers were lying in wait for me on the way. I think this not at all unlikely and although I know that everywhere I am in God's care and that not a hair of my head can be touched without his will, yet my heart is full of pity for my dear Katie, who would be half-dead with worry by the time I got back. So, don't be vexed that I cannot be at your wedding.'

A fortnight later Spalatin wrote: 'It has been discovered that four young noblemen were lying in wait for you, because you rescued their sisters from the convent and the brothers as a consequence are now having to support and endow them. Therefore, my friend, kiss your Katie's hand and thank her for, under God's guiding, she has kept you from danger.'

On the 8th June, 1526, there was glad news to report. 'My dear Katie presented me with a little Hans Luther yesterday at two o'clock, by God's grace. I must stop. Sick Katie is calling for me.' This was the crowning joy in a year of pure happiness for both. Soon Hans was cutting his teeth and letting everyone know about it. 'Such are the joys of marriage of which the Pope is not worthy!'

The second year of their life together was, by comparison, a black one. For one thing Luther was ill and depressed. In January he 'felt a rush of blood' to his heart and there were attacks of giddiness, possibly due to a middle ear infection which continued to trouble him. In July, thinking he was about to die, he commended Katie and little Hans to the care of God. 'My dear Katie, if it is God's will to take me, accept it. He will care for you and Hans.'

'My dear Doctor, as God pleases, I am willing that you should be with our Lord rather than with us. Don't worry about us. God will take care of us. But I am not just thinking of myself and Hans. There are so many people who need you.' Katie's serenity and fortitude must have put heart into her husband.

He recovered. Then the plague came to Wittenberg and the Elector ordered the University, students and staff, to move to Jena. With Bugenhagen and his assistant, Börer, Luther remained and opened his home to the ill and bereaved, among them Schurf, the doctor, and his family. His wife and Margaret von Mochau, a guest, were nursed by Katie and though Margaret's life hung in the balance they both slowly recovered.

A letter of August 15th says, 'Today we have buried Börer's wife who died yesterday almost in my arms. Justus Jonas has lost his son Johannes. I am staying on here as the people are in desperation.'

Four days later he wrote that the plague was weakening his faith. 'The pestilence has been three times in our house. My little son Hans has been ill for eight days and is being kept alive by liquids but now shows signs of recovering. For many months I have suffered from lack of faith. Pray that our faith may not fail. Katie sends money for linen and commends herself to your prayers.'

What made this year so bleak was the depression verging on panic from which Luther suffered –

the severest attack he had yet experienced. He had been subject to these *Anfechtungen*, as he called them, from his youth. Before becoming a monk he had been sad and melancholy and there were recurring attacks during his years in the monastery. No doubt various causative factors had different weight at different times. Tension, fastings, insomnia, overwork, diet and physical health may all have contributed something – though it is equally possible that his emotional state was the cause of some of his physical ailments. These *Anfechtungen* were times of overwhelming feelings of turmoil, desolation, lostness, alienation, spiritual malaise, amounting at their most intense to a 'horror of great darkness' which could not be endured for long.

They might take the form of self-doubt. Far from being an arrogant rebel glorying in the fight, it was only reluctantly and almost accidentally as it were that he found himself a spiritual leader. Never of those who dare not entertain the idea that they might be wrong, he could not be sure he was right till he had faced the possibility that he might be wrong, and faced it to the limit just as he had tested the monastic life to its limit and had given Popery every chance – even after Worms – to prove itself right. At Augsburg and again in the Wartburg the doubt that assailed him was precisely this – 'Are you alone right? *Bist du allein recht?* What if you are wrong and misleading others?' He was always testing the reality of what he stood for. It was not that he wrestled with self-doubt in order to overcome it; it was rather as though he gave the devil the benefit of the doubt, in order to test his own position. If he was indeed wrong he would need to find the truth; if he was right he could go forward with confidence.

It is sometimes difficult to distinguish, in Luther's thinking, between self-accusing thoughts and the insinuations of the devil. The general impression given is that doleful thoughts were provoked by the devil and both should be resisted. Such was his advice to others with the rueful comment, 'I can talk beautifully to you but I don't do so well myself.'

Worse by far than self-doubt or conflict with the devil were gnawing doubts about God himself. Is God indeed good? And if he is does he care? And, the crux of the matter, does he care about *me*? To feel far off from God – this was to be lost and alone, this was dereliction indeed.

On November 1st he wrote to Amsdorf, 'It seems to be God's will that I, who till now used to comfort you all, now need it greatly myself.' Hans was ill again and he was very anxious about Katie who was expecting their second child. The lives of both seemed in danger. He wrote to Justus Jonas, 'My Hans can send no greeting in his sickness but begs your prayers. For twelve days he had lived only on fluids but is now beginning to eat a little. The poor little fellow tries to play as he used to but is too weak.'

The truths he had preached to others seemed powerless to comfort himself.

'I do not believe that it is one devil that is attacking me but the very Prince of devils. So great is his power of assailing me with Scripture that my own knowledge of the Bible is not enough to protect and help me but I must be strengthened by words of Scripture out of the mouths of my friends. This is why I ask so earnestly for your prayers and if ever you are in the same case, the sport of the devil, you will understand my request.' Christ was wholly lost to him and he was 'shaken by desperation and blasphemy of God.'

No matter how long or severe his depressions might be, and they were to recur throughout his life, he still managed to get through an amazing amount of work. He felt that in some way they were inevitable if one were to have a real understanding of things spiritual, for 'he does not know what hope is who has never been subject to temptations.' At the same time they were to be avoided if at all possible. But how? As the spiritual pioneer of his age he could never look to others for affirmation nor could he ever find anything in himself on which to ground his hope. His affirmation must come from God but he could not know him directly, so in the final analysis he must be rooted in the Scriptures. That is why he gave such a priority to the translation of the Bible; it was so that each could find truth for himself. At other times he in his down-to-earth way said the best way to combat despondency was to go out among people, laugh, joke and sing; get involved, even get angry; do something useful such as harness the horse and spread manure on the fields. Music was especially effective for the devil is a morose being who flees music.

His *Anfechtungen* must have been a trial to Katie but her cheerfulness and common sense were equal to the situation. She would read to him from the Bible or send for Justus Jonas to come and cheer him up. As for her own faith the indications are that it was robust and uncomplicated. There would scarcely be room for two like Luther in the same house!

By year's end all was well. The plague had died down. On the 10th December a little girl was born and on the 29th Luther wrote to Justus Jonas, 'My Katie with little baby Elizabeth is well and sends you greetings but is longing to see you all here again in good health. Satan has again tried to drag me down into the abyss with powerful cart ropes and ships' cords but the weak Christ has as yet overcome through your prayers, and struggles for the victory.'

A fruit of that dreadful *Anfechtung* of 1527 was the hymn, with its tune, that is now sung round the world, *Ein' feste Burg ist unser Gott*.

A safe stronghold our God is still,
A trusty shield and weapon;
He'll help us clear from all the ill
That hath us now o'ertaken.
The ancient prince of hell
Hath risen with purpose fell;
Strong mail of craft and power
He weareth in this hour;
On earth is not his fellow.

With force of arms we nothing can,
Full soon were we down-ridden;
But for us fights the proper Man,
Whom God Himself hath bidden.
Ask ye: Who is this same?
Christ Jesus is His name,
The Lord Sabaoth's Son;
He, and no other one,
Shall conquer in the battle.

God's word, for all their craft and force,
One moment will not linger:
But, in spite of hell, shall have its course:
'Tis written by His finger.
And though they take our life,
Goods, honour, children, wife,
Yet is their profit small:
These things shall vanish all;
The City of God remaineth.

8

VINE AND OLIVES

Out through the Elster Gate and less than a quarter of a mile from the town was a well which Luther had discovered and renewed in 1520. There in 1526 he built a little summerhouse and often he and Katie relaxed there with their friends. While the children played together at hide-and-seek, blind man's bluff and the inevitable 'fighting', the grown-ups chatted and laughed, the women perhaps sewing or knitting as they joined in the general conversation or exchanged recipes and news.

There were trees, flowers, birds and butterflies to admire. Luther loved nature both for its beauty and for the thoughts it suggested. Of a rose he said, 'If a man could make one rose like this, people would say he was wonderful; yet God scatters hundreds around us.' The birds could teach us a thing or two. 'That little bird has chosen his shelter. Above are the stars and the deep vault of heaven. Yet there he is, rocking himself to sleep on his little twig without a care in the world, just leaving God to think for him.'

During those early years of his marriage Luther was engaged in translating the Old Testament and revising his translation of the New Testament. Indeed although the whole Bible was published in 1534 the work of revision never stopped. His aim was to make the meaning immediate and clear to the ordinary person so that each might judge for himself what was the truth, and in achieving it he recreated and enriched the German language. He listened to children at play and people at work; he gathered proverbs, folklore and songs, steeping himself in the language. Katie was an expert he said. He went to endless trouble to find the exact words he needed. One or two letters may be of interest.

To Spalatin: 'Be ready to supply us with the common names for some things, but not those used at court for this book is to be written in the simplest language that all may understand it. I need the names of the precious stones mentioned in Revelation 21. If only you could get permission from the Court to let us borrow some to see what they are like!'

Again: 'The translation of Job gives us immense trouble on account of its exalted language which seems to suffer even more under our attempts to translate it than ever Job did under the consolation of his friends. It seems to prefer to lie among the ashes. Evidently the author didn't wish it to be translated.'

His aim, he said, was to make Moses so German that no one would suspect he was a Jew.

As well as translating the Scriptures, he was engaged in preaching and exposition. The Epistle to the Galatians was a special favourite of his, 'my Catherine von Bora' he called it .

Besides his translating, lecturing, preaching, composing and writing he kept up a vast correspondence. (It is good for us that the 16th century was telephone-free.) Luther's letters sparkle with allusions to his Katie. A picture emerges of her flitting in and out of the study.

'Have you written to Nicholas yet?'

'Remember to thank him for the quincy juice.'

'Tell them I wish them all joy in their marriage and in his new post,' and he duly did. At the end of letters berating the Pope and the Devil come playful references through which shines his affection for his family. 'Many greetings from my Katie, the head of the house. Greet your wife who may be your lord also' was, as likely as not, written for Katie's benefit. She often sat beside him for he consulted her about his correspondence and she helped whenever she could. 'Katie is having little books bound to send to your dear daughters as a remembrance. She is always praising your kindness.'

Once he wrote to a composer thanking him for a song (and apples):

'We sing as well as we can at table and continue afterwards. If we make mistakes after going over the same tune three or four times don't on any account blame us; blame our meagre talent. Even if composers make first-class tunes we manage to improve them.' Katie must have peeped over his shoulder for he added, 'Katie hopes you will not take this joking amiss and sends you kindly greetings.'

Toddler Hans might be at his knee. 'Give your wife my thanks. My Katie and I hope that she and her child will live happy in Christ. My little prattling Hans must also send his respects to you.' We can almost see him rescuing the letter from smudging fingers as he stops for a chat with the little fellow.

In August their *liebe Elisabeth* grew pale and wan and in spite of all Katie's skill and care she died. She had brightened their home for less than eight months. On her grave was set up a small wooden cross carved by Luther's faithful servant, Wolfgang, and bearing the inscription, *Hic dormit Elisabeth filiola Martini Lutheri Anno 1528.* (Here sleeps Elizabeth, Martin Luther's little daughter.)

On 5th August, Luther wrote to Hausmann, 'My Hanschen thanks you, dear Nicolas, for the rattle which he is very proud of. My little daughter Elizabeth has been taken away from me, leaving me strangely sick at heart, almost like a woman so deeply am I grieved. I would never have believed that a father's heart could be so tender towards his children.'

Katie was inconsolable and it took her a long time to get over the loss.

In the following May their third child was born and Luther wrote to Amsdorf in such excitement that the pen squirted and scratched.

'Grace and peace, my dear friend Amsdorf! God has looked on us in our sorrow and has graciously given us a little daughter in place of the one who was taken, so I pray you come with all speed that she may not remain a heathen but that her name may, through her baptism, be entered as an heir of the life everlasting.' She was called Magdalena and was her father's favourite, perhaps because her coming helped to assuage his grief, or perhaps because she took after her mother in looks – or more likely because of her own sweet nature. She was a delightful child, gentle, obedient and loving, the sunshine of the home and brother Hans' devoted admirer.

There were three children more – Martin, born on 9th November, 1531; Paul, born on 18th January, 1533; and Margaretha, born on 17th December, 1534. Martin's birthday was just two days before the feast of St Martin (and the day before his father's). Paul was called after the great apostle to whom Luther (and through him, Katie) owed so much.

At the beginning of October, Luther, Melancthon and Justus Jonas were at a conference in Marburg where the leading Swiss and German theologians were endeavouring to reach agreement on a common confession. The letter which Luther wrote to Katie on the 4th shows that she was not merely on the fringe of the Reformation but took an informed interest in the questions of the day.

'Dear Katie,

'Our friendly conference at Marburg is almost ended, and we have agreed upon all points except that our opponents maintain that only the bread and wine are present in the sacraments although admitting Christ's spiritual presence in the elements. Today the Landgrave is making every effort to unite us or at least to make us consider each other as brothers and members of Christ's body. Although we object to being brothers, we wish to live at peace and on good terms. Say to Herr Pommer that Zwingli's argument was the best: "Corpus non potest esse sine loco, ergo Christi corpus non est in pane." That of Oecolampadius was, "Sacramentum est signum corporis Christi."

'Goodnight to all and pray for us. We are all well and lively, and living like princes. Kiss Lenchen and Hanschen for me.

Your obedient servant, Martin Luther.

P.S. They are all quite excited over the sweating sickness. Fifty were seized yesterday, of whom two have died.'

Not a very reassuring postscript! However, he reached home hale and hearty.

In February news came from his brother James in Mansfeld that their father was seriously ill. He and the mother had been to Wittenberg on holiday and had been accorded great honour by the citizens. It is cheering to think of old Hans being presented with a *vin d'honneur* and playing with his little grandson. During their visit in 1527 they had had their portraits painted by Cranach. On the 16th Luther wrote:

'It would be a great joy to us if only you and Mother would come here. My Katie and all of us beg you with tears; we would nurse you tenderly. I have sent Cyriac to see if you are able, for I should like to be near you so that I might care for you.

'I commit you to him who loves you better than you do yourself, having paid the penalty of your sins with his blood, so that you need have no anxiety. Leave him to see to everything. May this dear Saviour be with you, and we shall shortly meet again with Christ. The departure from this world is a much smaller thing with God than if I said goodbye to you in Mansfeld to come here, or if you took your leave of me in Wittenberg to go back to Mansfeld. It is one hour's sleep and all is changed.

'My Katie, Hanschen, Lenchen, Aunt Lene all greet you and pray for you. Give our love to my dear mother and all the relations.

'Your dear son, Martin.'

Cyriac was a nephew who was staying with the Luthers at this time. Hans was apparently unable to face the journey; at any rate he did not come.

In April Luther had to leave Wittenberg on account of the Diet of Augsburg at which the Emperor Charles V and the Papal Legate were to confer with the Protestant Princes, their object being to induce the latter to submit to the Catholic faith. Luther and Melancthon had drawn up a Confession but the Elector was concerned for Luther's safety, for he was still under the ban of the Emperor, and would not allow him to go to Augsburg. Melancthon was to head the Protestant delegation while Luther stayed in Coburg Castle, out of reach of danger but near enough to advise. It was like the Wartburg all over again but not for so long – six months from April 1530 – and not quite so lonely for he had Cyriac and his secretary, Veit Dietrich, with him. As the weeks dragged on the inactivity and loneliness of life in the empty castle told on his health and spirits. He sent for his books and busied himself with his commentaries.

On 5th June he received word that his father had died on the 29th May and he wrote that same day to his close friend, Melancthon:

'My beloved father, old Hans Luther, died at one on Sabbath morning. His death has cast me into deep grief, not only because he was my father, but because it was through his great love to me that my Creator endowed me with all I am and have and although I am comforted to learn that he gently fell asleep in Christ Jesus, strong in faith, yet his loss has caused a deep wound in my heart. I am too sad to write more today, and it is only right to mourn such a father, who by the sweat of his brow made me what I am.'

His letter to his mother is full of spiritual consolation and loving advice.

While he was away the whole responsibility of the home devolved on Katie and it says much for her that Luther was able to go away for such a long period with a free mind. She never lost sight of the fact that he was a public figure and belonged first to God and then to the world of Christians who depended on him. Therefore she never grudged his absences but set to, to make things at home as comfortable and happy as she could so that he could give himself wholeheartedly to the work to which he was called. 'I am too apt to expect more from my Katie than I do from Christ my Lord, though he has done so much more for me,' he once remarked and it worried him.

Besides their own children they had staying with them at some time or another eleven orphans, children of Luther's sisters, among them Elsa and Lene Kaufmann and Hans' tutors, Peter and Hieronymous Weller. Katie's Aunt Lene, who had been with her at the convent, also stayed with them. Then Luther gladly took the opportunity to repay the friends of his Eisenach days by taking into his home Henry Cotta, a grandson of Conrad and Ursula. Like many of the University staff he had students boarding with him and they were treated as part of the family. Naturally Katie could not look after such a household without help, even though she was up by five every morning, so there were servants, too, to cater for – and they could cause problems. On one occasion Luther was writing to Link to whose wife they had sent a gift.

> 'You order me or my Katie to say what we wish in return. If you are determined to send something, let it be a lamp, but not a common one, such as we used as monks, but one that can carry two or three candles; and let it be strong enough to stand all the knocks it may get in cleaning, or when thrown downstairs or even only sent on in advance; better still if you could find one that does not need cleaning (for you know the idle ways of servants nowadays) then it would be safe against the ill-treatment of the maids when they are in the sulks or have a fit of laziness.'

As well as the permanent residents in the monastery, there were the numerous guests they entertained for their home was a haven of hospitality to those in need, among them Elizabeth, wife of the Elector of Brandenburg, one of the Catholic Princes. She was a sister of King Christian of Denmark and, like him, a warm admirer of Luther. On hearing that she had been present at a celebration of the Lord's Supper in which the communicants had partaken of both the bread and the wine her husband had locked her in her room and sworn that she would never again see the light of sun or moon till she recanted. Disguised as a peasant she escaped one night and made for her uncle's castle at Torgau. He, none other than the Elector of Saxony and Luther's friend, made her welcome and granted her the castle of Lichtenburg not far from Wittenberg. She often sent for Luther whose help she greatly valued and, in turn, visited his home even staying for one or two months. She and Katie became firm friends and she was Magdalena's godmother. Unhappily there was never a reconciliation between the prince and herself.

It was perhaps as well for Katie that her hands were full for there was certainly no time for self-pity. She did find time to think of her grieving husband, however, and casting about for a way of bringing some warmth and cheer to his desolated spirit she had Cranach paint a portrait of Magdalena, then one year old, and sent it to him. Soon she received a letter from Dietrich.

'Dear and gracious Mrs Luther:
'Rest assured that your lord is in good health and spirits as we too are by God's grace. It was a good idea to send the doctor the portrait for it takes his mind off his worries. He has hung it on the wall opposite the table at which we eat in the Prince's

apartment. At first he could scarcely recognise her and said, "Lenchen is not as dark as that," but he now sees that it is indeed Lenchen and likes it more and more. She is very like Hans in the mouth, eyes and nose; in fact there is a strong resemblance altogether and she will come to look even more like him. I felt I must write to let you know this.

'You need not be concerned about the doctor. He is in good heart, praise God. The news of his father's death upset him at first but after two days he was himself again. When the letter came he said, "My father is dead." He picked up his psalter and took to his room where we heard him weeping. For two days he could do nothing at all but he has been fine since. God be with Hans and Lenchen and the whole household.'

There were letters from Luther for he kept in close touch. One, dated 19th June, was for four-year-old Hans whose playmates were the sons of Melancthon and Jonas.

'My dear little son:

'I am glad you are working hard at your lessons and are praying too. Keep on my boy, and when I come home I shall bring something from the fair.

'I know a lovely garden where many children, dressed all in gold, gather rosy apples under the trees as well as pears and plums and cherries. They dance and sing as merry as the day is long. They have fine little ponies with golden reins and silver saddles. I asked the gardener who these children were and he said, "These are the children who like to pray and learn and be good." I said, "Sir, I too have a son and his name is Hans Luther: couldn't he come into the garden too and eat the apples and pears and ride on a fine pony, and play with the children?" And the man said, "If he likes to pray and learn and be good he too may come into the garden – and Lippus and Jost also; and when they all come together they shall have golden whistles and drums and lutes; and they'll dance about and shoot with silver bows and arrows."

'And he showed me a lawn all ready for dancing. But it was early, and the children had not yet had breakfast, so I couldn't wait for the dance. I said to the man, "I must go straight away and write all this to my dear son Hans so that he will be sure to pray and work hard and be good so that he too may come into this garden. But he has an Aunt Lene: he'll have to bring her too." "That will be all right," said the man. "Write and tell him so."

'So, my darling son, learn your lessons and say your prayers and tell Lippus and Jost to do so too, so that you may all come together into the garden. May the good God take care of you. Give my love to Aunt Lene and give her a kiss from me.

Your loving father,
Martin Luther.'

On the 15th August came a letter addressed,

'To my dearest Katie Luther at Wittenberg.
'Grace and peace in Christ, my dear Katie! After closing your letter, I received letters from Augsburg, so I detained the messenger to let him take them with him.

'You will see things remain much the same in Augsburg as I described them lately. Let Peter Weller and Herr Pommer read them to you. May God graciously continue to help us. I can't write more at the moment as the messenger is losing patience. Greet our dear Sack and Hans Luther, and his tutor, to whom I shall write shortly. Greet Aunt Lene, and all the rest. We are eating ripe grapes although we have had a lot of rain this month. God be with you all. Amen.

From the desert.'

On the 15th September he wrote, 'I have a lovely large sugar book for Hanschen Luther.'

Letters went the other way too, sometimes with requests from Katie which were faithfully passed on as the one to Link in Nürnberg on 27th June, 'If you can procure from your good friends five dozen oranges for my Catherine, I shall gladly pay for them as there are none in Wittenberg.'

After six long months Luther was home once more and we can be sure there was much jollity in the old monastery. Before long there was sad news from Mansfeld – his mother was ill, and it proved to be her last illness. On 20th May, 1531, Luther wrote her a long letter of spiritual comfort and encouragement ending, 'All your children pray for you, also my Katie. Some of us weep; others eat and say, "Grannie is very ill." May the grace of God be with us all. Amen.'

*****

One can picture the chubby little ones sitting at table and nodding wisely as they echo the grown-ups' talk. With the household at times numbering as many as twenty-five, mealtimes must have been rather noisy occasions, and rather comical for the student boarders came down to dinner armed with notebooks in which they scribbled down all the words of wisdom and unwisdom that the great man uttered. Only Luther could have stood it. Katie laughed and said they should pay for the privilege. These sayings, almost seven thousand in all, have been collated and published under the name of *Table Talk*. Prised from their context though they are, they yet give a fascinating glimpse into the range of subjects that figured in the usually free-flowing conversation.

Asked why he was at times so violent Luther said, 'A twig can be cut with a breadknife, but for an oak you need an axe.'

Someone sent to know whether it was permissible to use warm water in baptism. 'Tell the blockhead that water, warm or cold, is water.'

'Our Lord God is like a printer, who sets the letters backwards, so that here that is the way we must read them; when we are printed off yonder, in the life to come, we shall read all clear and straightforward.'

'Botchers think everything they do is perfect.'

'The ungodly abuse the gospel and are made worse so it is not the gospel but the law that

95

belongs to them. Just as when my little Hans does something wrong if I didn't spank him but gave him sugar-plums he would be quite spoilt.'

With guests there might on occasion be as many as a hundred at the table. The main meal was usually served at five o'clock. After dinner there would be games. Luther had a bowling-alley built at the back of the monastery and often led the game himself. He believed in jollity. 'No one knows how it hurts a young man to avoid happiness and to cultivate solitude and melancholy. I, who have spent my life in mourning, now seek and accept joy wherever I can find it.'

On summer evenings there would be conversation under the pear tree and always the music that he loved, that 'fair and lovely gift of God' which drives away the devil and makes people happy. 'My heart sings and overflows with joy in response to music which has so often refreshed me.' Walther, the composer with whom he sometimes worked, got the impression that he would never weary of singing or feel he had had enough of it. He had a sweet tenor voice and there was nothing he enjoyed more than those after-dinner sing-songs with family and friends for while he loved music he loved music-and-children more. To the accompaniment of harp or flute they sang folk songs, hymns and psalms. Some of the hymns were composed by the head of the house himself, quite possibly specifically for his own children. One of the loveliest is the fresh and childlike, *Von Himmel Hoch* ('From heaven above to earth I come' in Catherine Winkworth's translation). A little carol shows Luther's unique blend of the homely and the sublime:

Our little Lord, we give thee praise
That thou hast deigned to take our ways.
Born of a maid a man to be,
And all the angels sing to thee.

The eternal Father's Son he lay
Cradled in the crib of hay.
The everlasting God appears
In our frail flesh and blood and tears.

What the globe could not enwrap
Nestled lies in Mary's lap.
Just a baby, very wee,
Yet Lord of all the world is he.

In 1524 Luther had brought out a hymn book in which over twenty of the hymns were by himself – words and sometimes the music – and all Germany was singing them.

He took great pleasure in his children and loved to watch them at play. Their innocent, carefree spontaneity spoke to his heart as did their matter-of-fact, unquestioning trust in God.

Dr Jonas invited him to dinner one day and over the table hung a bunch of ripe cherries as a suggestion to his guests to praise God for creating such fruits. Luther's response was,

'Shouldn't our children rather call such praise from us? They are always before our eyes and after all we can learn more from them than from a cherry bough.' In writing to his friends he would send greetings to their 'vine and olive plants', an allusion to Psalm 128, where the poet tells the God-fearing man, 'Your wife shall be like a fruitful vine growing beside your house, your children like olive plants round your table.'

He believed children should be taught to approach God with confidence as a loving Father. If conscious of having done wrong they should be encouraged to ask at once for forgiveness. For their instruction he drew up the *Children's Catechism*, a simple affirmation of faith, which was to be taught in the home. The booklet was made attractive-looking with charming woodcuts. One or two excerpts give the flavour of this little work that Luther considered one of the best things he wrote. '"Our Father who art in heaven." What does this mean?'

'God will in this way gently persuade us to believe that he is our true Father, and that we are his true children; that cheerfully and with all confidence we may ask of him as dear children ask of their dear fathers.'

'What does Amen mean?'

'That I should be sure such prayers are acceptable to the Father in heaven, and granted by him for he himself has taught us thus to pray and promised that he will hear us.'

Every day the whole household gathered for prayers when some verses from the Bible were read and explained and a psalm or hymn was sung.

When away on his necessary travels the father's thoughts were continually winging homewards. In February 1532 he wrote asking Katie to give a gift to a servant who was retiring:

'You know how faithful he has been, putting up with everything, so do not let him want for anything. I would gladly give him ten gulden if I had them – but under five you must not go, for his clothing is worn and thin. Please give him more if you can. Kiss little Hans and tell him, Lenchen and Aunt Lene to pray for the dear Prince and me. I can find nothing for the children here although it is the Fair so have something ready if I bring nothing special.'

In July, 1534 he was away again. 'You must wonder how long I am likely to stay or, rather, how long you will be rid of me. I keep thinking what good wine and beer I have at home, as well as a beautiful wife, or shall I say lord?'

In 1537 Aunt Lene was ill and Luther assured her, 'You will not die but sleep away as in a cradle, and when the morning dawns you will rise and live forever.' She was greatly missed for she was loved by one and all.

His letters are Luther's monument to his love for Katie. Katie's monument to her love took the form of a doorway! It was designed with help from Lucas Cranach and built as a surprise for her husband on one of his homecomings. Intricately carved in sandstone it has on one side a sculpture of her husband and on the other, not one of herself, but of his crest. On it was the date 1540.

In that year Katie was seriously ill and Luther cried, 'Oh Katie, do not die and leave me!' She gradually recovered, seemingly from the brink of the grave, so that he was able to write in March, 'My Katie's appetite is returning, and she is able to get around slowly by holding on to the tables and chairs.'

By midsummer all was well. Luther was again from home and wrote, 'Grace and peace, dear Katie! Your Grace must know that, God be praised, we are here fresh and well, eat like Bohemians and drink like Germans – but in moderation – and are full of joy.'

9

SAINTS TO HEAVEN

In 1540 Luther bought for Katie a small estate on the road to Altenburg, near Leipzig. The house was in need of repair which suited Katie's creative energies perfectly. It belonged to a relative of hers who had fallen into debt, probably her brother Hans for in the following year Luther wrote to the Elector asking for a post 'however small' for him. 'He is faithful and pious, that I know, also active and industrious but he has not enough to keep himself and his child. He was superintendent of a monastery in Leipzig and although they tried to malign him his accounts were found to be correct and his enemies' mouths were shut. I made them admit this.'

Luther felt his strength waning and wanted Katie to be well provided for in the event of his death.

She was delighted with the estate and got Luther to order oak 'not the brushwood but the thicker stems. She wishes them for the fireplaces in her new property. We shall pay for what is needed so that the new proprietress may have her kingdom suitably fitted out.' Three years later she was still busy. 'She is sending her horses and carts to fetch the remaining pieces of wood while the weather and roads are good.' It was a haven of rest and peace for the whole family.

In 1542 Hans was sixteen and since there was not a good school in Wittenberg he had to go to Torgau for the next stage of his education. In spite of Luther's talk about the need for discipline, all had not gone smoothly with his upbringing; he had perhaps had more sugar-plums than spankings! Luther's letter of 26th August to Marcus Crödel, the teacher, reads:

> 'I send you my son Hans, my dear Marcus, so that he may be instructed in grammar and music and at the same time I hope you will attend to his manners and morals. I am committing a great trust to you in the Lord. God bless your efforts. If they are successful I shall, if spared, send the other two boys. Say to Hans Weller that I pray for him and commit my little son to his care for music. I can train theologians, but I wish my children to have grammar and music.'

Poor Hans, he had hardly settled in when another letter arrived for his teacher.

> 'Please don't tell my son Hans what I am about to write. My daughter Magdalena is nearing her end and will soon go to her true Father in heaven unless he sees fit to spare her. She longs so much to see her brother, for they were very close, so I

am sending a carriage for him, in the hope that a sight of him will revive her. I'm doing all I can lest afterwards the thought of having neglected anything should torment me. Please ask him to come home at once, without telling him why. I shall send him back as soon as she has either fallen asleep in the Lord or been restored to health. Farewell in the Lord. Say to him that we must have something private to tell him. All here are otherwise well.'

Magdalena so blithe, so gentle, was just thirteen but neither the care of the doctors nor Katie's skilful nursing could restore the bloom of health. She died bravely and trustingly as children often do.

'Oh God,' Luther prayed, 'I love her dearly but thy will be done.' And turning to her,

'Magdalena, my little girl, you would like to stay with your father here and you would as gladly go to your Father in heaven?'

'Yes, dearest father, as God wills.'

And Luther grieved that although God had blessed him as no bishop had been blessed in a thousand years, yet he could not find it in his heart to give God thanks.

The night before her death Katie, from sheer exhaustion, fell asleep and dreamed that two young men, splendidly attired, came to conduct her darling child to her wedding – and read hope into the dream.

As the end drew near Luther fell on his knees at her bedside praying with tears that God would receive his dear one, while Katie stood at the far side of the room unable to watch her child as she died in her father's arms. Then he turned to console the weeping mother.

'Dearest Katie, let us think of the home our daughter has gone to; there she is happy and at peace.'

When she was laid in her coffin he said, 'My darling Lenchen, you will rise and shine like the stars and the sun. How strange to know that she is at peace and all is well and yet to be sorrowful!' and to his friends who came to weep with them,

'Let us not be sad. I have sent a saint to heaven. If mine could be like hers I would gladly welcome death at this very hour.'

She was buried beside her sister, Elizabeth, in the churchyard and Luther wrote an epitaph.

> Here I, Magdalena,
> Doctor Luther's little maid
> Resting with the saints
> Sleep in my narrow bed
> I was a child of death
> For I was born in sin
> But now I live, redeemed Lord Christ,
> By the blood you shed for me.

She died shortly after nine o'clock on the 20th September and three days later the heartbroken father wrote to Justus Jonas who had moved to Halle.

'I expect you have heard that my beloved Magdalena has been born again into Christ's everlasting kingdom. Although my wife and I ought to rejoice because of her happy end, yet such is the strength of natural affection that we cannot think of it without sobs and groans which tear the heart apart. The memory of her face, her words, her expression, in life and in death – everything about our most obedient and loving daughter lingers in our hearts so that even the death of Christ (and what are all deaths compared to his?) is almost powerless to lift our minds above our loss. So would you give thanks to God in our stead? For hasn't he honoured us greatly in glorifying our child? You know how gentle and sweet she was, how altogether lovely. Christ be praised who chose her and called her and has now glorified her. I pray God that I and all of us may have such a death, yes and such a life.'

On 25th December there was another letter to his friend on the death of his wife, Katie's dearest friend.

'I have been so prostrated by this unexpected calamity that I do not know what to write. We have all lost in her the dearest of friends. Her bright and trusting personality won our love especially as we knew she shared our joys and sorrows as if they had been her own. I had hoped that after I was gone she would have been the comfort of those I left behind. We, after mourning a little while, shall enter into joy as your Katie and my Magdalena have. My wife was thunderstruck when she heard the news for she and your wife were as one. You have good cause to rejoice as she fell asleep in Jesus, with so many expressions of her faith in him. So also slept my little daughter, which is my great and only consolation.'

By this time Hans had returned to Torgau but, homesick and heart-broken, all he wanted was to be back in the family circle in Wittenberg.

At the end of December there was a letter from home.

'Grace and peace, my dearest Hans! Your mother and I and all of us are well. Do try to be brave and dry up your tears so that you won't add to your mother's distress for she is only too ready to feel sad. Obey God who, through us, is asking you to go on working where you are and then you will find it easier to overcome your grief. Your mother cannot write just now; she doesn't think she needs to repeat what she has already said to you - that you can come home if things go too badly with you, but she meant if you were ill. In that case, let us know at once. Otherwise she hopes you will dry up you tears and take fresh heart and go quietly on with your studies. May all go well with you in the Lord.'

That must have been a sad year's end for the young brothers and sister – Martin twelve, Paul almost ten and Margaretha just turned eight.

Luther himself never got over Magdalena's death. His health deteriorated and he began to regard himself, prematurely perhaps, as an 'old exhausted man.' His head was 'like a knife, from which the steel is wholly whetted away and is become mere iron; the iron will cut no more; so it is with my head.' In January, 1546, we have, 'I, old, weary, lazy, worn out, cold, chilly and, over and above, with only one eye to see with now write you ...' But still he was servant to all who needed him. He had written, 'I will give myself as a kind of Christ to my neighbour as Christ gave himself for me' and he lived up to it. Towards the end of 1545 he was asked to go to Eisleben, his birthplace, to settle a dispute between the Counts of Mansfeld over the mines. He was unsuccessful and was invited again in January. Before leaving home, this time accompanied by his three sons and Justus Jonas, he said he could lie down on his death bed with joy if only he could just see his dear Lords of Mansfeld reconciled. He had just finished his commentary on Genesis, laying down his pen with the words, 'I am weak and can do no more. Pray God he may grant me a peaceful and happy death.' Katie packed medicines for him for he was not feeling well and she sent solicitous letters after him.

Replies were not long in coming.

15th January, 1546.
'To my kind and dear Katie Luther at Wittenberg, grace and peace in the Lord.' (This was the address on the outside).

'Dear Katie,

Today at half past eight we reached Halle, but have not yet reached Eisleben for a great anabaptist met us with flood waters and great blocks of ice, covering the land and threatening to baptise us all again. We couldn't go back because of the Hulda so we are staying peacefully here at Halle between the two streams. I would not have believed that the Saale could make such a brewing, bursting over the causeway and all. I believe if you had been here you would have advised us to do precisely what we have done, so for once we should have taken your advice.'

Katie got used to having letters addressed, *on the outside*, as the next one was:

'To my dearly beloved housewife, Katherin Lutherin, owner of Zulsdorf and the Pigmarket and whatever else she may be, grace and peace in Christ; and my old, poor and (as I am aware) powerless love to you!'

This one was signed 'Martin Luther, your old lover.'

A few days later he wrote, 'Pray, read, dear Katie, the Gospel of St John and the little Catechism of which you once declared that you yourself had said all that it contained.' She was not to be anxious as though God could not raise up new Martin Luthers by the dozen for the old one drowned in the Saale!

10th February, 1546.
'To the saintly, anxious lady, Katherine Luther, owner of Zulsdorf, at Wittenberg, my gracious dear wife. Grace and peace in Christ.

'Most saintly lady doctor, we thank you kindly for your great concern for us which prevented your sleeping, for since you began to be so anxious about us we have been nearly consumed by a fire in our inn, just outside my door: and yesterday (no doubt due to your anxiety) a stone almost fell on our heads and crushed us as in a mouse-trap: for in our bedroom lime and mortar kept coming down for two days and when the workmen came they just touched it with two fingers and down fell a stone as large as a pillow. We had your anxious care to thank for all this, but fortunately the dear, holy angels guarded us too. I'm afraid that if you do not stop being so worried the earth may eventually swallow us up. Is this the way you've learned the catechism? Pray and leave God to look after us as he has promised. Cast your burden on the Lord and he shall sustain you. We would gladly be free and set out on our homeward journey, God willing. Amen, Amen, Amen.

Your obedient servant, Martin Luther.'

Then came news of his homecoming.

14th February, 1546.
'To my dear sweet wife, Katherine Luther, at Wittenberg. Grace and peace in the Lord!
'Dear Katie,
We hope to be with you this week, God willing. God has richly manifested his grace towards us here

for the lords have come to an agreement, except on two or three points, one of which is that the two brothers, Counts Gebhardt and Albrecht, should again become brothers which I shall try to bring about today by inviting them to be my guests – so that they will speak to each other instead of embittering each other with letters.

'Our young nobles are all for gaiety now, riding out together on sledges to the tinkling of fools' bells; and the young ladies go too, all joking and in high spirits.

'From this one may see that God is the hearer of prayer.

'I send you some trout, which the Countess Albrecht has sent me. She is delighted with the reconciliation.

'Your sons are still at Mansfeld. Jacob Luther will look after them well. We are provided with meat and drink like lords, and have every attention paid us – indeed too much, so that we might forget you in Wittenberg. I have no ailments.'

It was not to be. On the very day he wrote that letter he preached his last sermon, in Eisleben, breaking off with the words; 'Much more might be said about the Gospel but I am too weak. We will leave off here.' By the 17th, a Wednesday, he was so ill that the Counts persuaded him to rest indoors. In the afternoon he felt a pain at his heart but recovered sufficiently to join the company for supper in the Great Hall where the conversation touched on all manner of subjects but especially on death and eternity. He was cheerful, even gay. On retiring to his room he again felt pain and had warm cloths brought to ease it. It was clear that he was seriously ill. Count Albrecht himself brought him medicine but it did not help. Soon he fell asleep watched anxiously by Paul and Martin who had come back from Mansfeld and stayed with him all night. Justus Jonas and some twelve other friends waited and kept the fire up.

When he awoke and saw their anxious faces he said, 'Are you still here? Go, my friends, and rest yourselves.'

Again he drifted off to sleep and when he next opened his eyes Jonas asked him how he felt.

'I am very ill. I think I shall remain here at Eisleben; here where I was born and baptised.'

Later he repeated three times, 'Father, into thine hand I commit my spirit: thou hast redeemed me, Lord God of truth.'

For the consolation of his followers Jonas asked, 'Do you die trusting in Christ and the doctrines you have preached?' and all heard the unhesitating 'Yes.'

He fell asleep and went, a saint, to heaven between two and three o'clock on the morning of Thursday, 18th February. He was sixty-two.

When he heard of the death of his boyhood hero and lifelong friend, the Elector of Saxony requested that the body be taken to Wittenberg. On the Friday Justus Jonas preached in St Andrew's Church and at noon on Saturday the coffin was carried with great solemnity to the gates of Eisleben followed by a large crowd including princes (among them a prince of Anhalt), nobles, schoolchildren and peasants. Surely there was never a funeral procession like it. In front rode a troop of fifty cavalry under the command of the sons of the Counts. In all the villages on the way the church bells tolled and at every crossroads groups of weeping people paid tribute to the brave, unselfish man who had shown them how to live and how to die. In Halle the body rested overnight in the Church of our Lady of which Justus Jonas was now the pastor.

On Monday the 22nd they were met at the Elster Gate by all Wittenberg and the procession then made its way towards the Castle Church at the far end of the town. Preachers and scholars led the way singing, while behind the wagon bearing the coffin rode Katie and Margaretha in a carriage, followed by her three sons and their Uncle James with other relatives. Behind rode the Elector and nobles, then came a carriage in which sat Justus Jonas, Bugenhagen and Melancthon. 'Lastly,' says an old manuscript, 'followed a verye greate Nomber of Matrons, Virgines and Children' all weeping. In the church Bugenhagen preached 'a moste Sweete and Godly Sermone' based on the words, 'I would not have you ignorant, brethren, concerning them which are asleep that you sorrow not as others which have no hope', followed by a funeral oration by Philip Melancthon. Katie and the four children wept as though alone in that great church as Luther's body was laid to rest near that door on which he had nailed his theses more than twenty-eight years before.

In her deep grief Katie no doubt recalled the affirmations and pleadings of Psalm 31 which Luther had made her memorise when she was young and buoyant so that she might be strengthened in the day of trouble.

> In thee, O Lord, do I put my trust;
> let me never be ashamed:
> deliver me in thy righteousness.
> Bow down thine ear to me;
> deliver me speedily:
> be thou my strong rock, for an house of
>   defence to save me.
> For thou art my rock and my fortress;
> therefore for thy name's sake lead me
>   and guide me.
> Pull me out of the net that they have
>   laid privily for me:
> for thou art my strength.
> Into thy hand I commit my spirit:
> thou hast redeemed me, O Lord God of truth.

and the ringing finale:

> Be of good courage,
> and he shall strengthen your heart,
> all ye that hope in the Lord.

She needed all her courage as she and the family tried to adjust to their great loss. Letters of consolation from ministers and princes helped as did the sympathy of people from all walks of life.

Luther's will, drawn up on the 6th January, 1542, reflects his great love for Katie. He left to his 'dear and faithful wife, Catherine,' all his property including 'all silver goblets and other valuables such as rings, chains, and medals of gold and silver.' He gave three reasons: 'first, my Catherine has always been a gentle, pious and faithful wife to me, has loved me dearly and by the grace of God has given me and brought up five children still living: second, she will have to settle any debts outstanding at the time of my death: third, and most important, it is my wish that the children be dependent on her, not she upon the children, that they honour her and be submissive to her as God has commanded. I consider, moreover, that the mother will be the best guardian of her children and that she will not abuse this confidence I place in her but will always be a good mother to her children whom she loves tenderly, and will conscientiously share everything with them.' He went on to beg his friends to defend his 'dear Catherine' against any slanders, for the devil might well want to have a thrust at her.

Catherine and the children might have been comfortably provided for through the kindness of patrons (the Elector, the Counts of Mansfeld and Christian III of Denmark all promised help) had not the outbreak of the long-dreaded Schmalkald War between the Emperor and the Protestant Princes diverted their attention. Hans was a student at Königsberg University but Martin and Paul were being educated at home as, of course, was Gretchen.

Catherine's grief finds expression in a letter she wrote on the 25th of April to her sister-in-law, Christine:

'That you have a heart-felt sympathy with me and my poor children I can readily believe for who would not be grieved and full of sorrow over such a precious man as was my dear husband, who served well not a town only or even a country but the whole world. And in truth so painful has been my grief that I cannot express to any my heart-suffering. I don't really know what I think or feel. I can neither eat or drink nor can I sleep. If I had had an earldom or a kingdom I would not have felt their loss so deeply as now when our dear Lord God has taken from me, and not from me only but from the whole world, this dear and well-loved man. When I think about it I can, for sorrow and weeping (as God well knows), neither speak nor write.'

In December, 1546 they had to take refuge for a short time in Magdeburg when Wittenberg was under siege. By the following April the Elector was taken prisoner and Charles was approaching Wittenberg with the intention, it was rumoured, of destroying the city where Luther preached. So once again they made for Magdeburg where one of the town councillors made them welcome. Then Magdeburg was threatened for sheltering refugees from Wittenberg and they moved to Brunswick. By this time Catherine felt that nowhere in the Emperor's domain would she find a place of rest but perhaps if they could reach Denmark ...

Just then there was a proclamation inviting the citizens of Wittenburg to return. The story goes that Lucas Cranach had years before done a portrait of the Emperor and in spite of the fact that the young boy was a troublesome, restless sitter, it had turned out well. Delighted, the prince had shaken his hand saying, 'Master Cranach, when I am a prince like my uncle and you want anything you have only to ask me and you shall have it.' The time had now come to hold him to that promise, thought Cranach, so when granted an audience he asked that the Emperor should treat the Elector with kindness. The city was spared but not the Elector whose courage and faith throughout five long years proved him a worthy follower of his spiritual leader. His wife, Sybilla of Cleves (a sister of Henry VIII's wife), charming and witty and a warm friend of Catherine, now moved to Weimar.

When Katie returned to Wittenberg she was relieved to find that her husband's grave had not been violated. Urged to scatter the heretic's bones to the four winds, the Emperor had replied, 'I wage war with the living, not the dead.'

Katie was now nearly penniless. Heavy war taxes were imposed which she could not meet, the more so that the beloved farm at Zulsdorf lay right in the path of war. Her friends rallied round but they, too, were poor and found the crippling taxes a burden. Practical as ever she did what she could. She let some of her apartments and boarded students. She wrote to the King of Denmark – on three occasions – but received no reply. This must have been hurtful for he had been a staunch supporter of Luther and still sent financial support to Melancthon and Bugenhagen who also wrote on her behalf but with equal lack of success. If she had indeed been proud before she was now having to learn humility. Goblet after goblet had to be sold to maintain the family. All the children were with her except Hans who was now working and whose cheery letters they looked forward to.

Then early in 1552 Bugenhagen heard that there was a possibility that the letters to Denmark had never arrived and urged Katie to write once more, which she did reminding his most Sovereign Majesty that he had been in the habit of sending her husband an honorarium .... 'I am forced, by distress, to apply to your Royal

Highness in the urgent hope that your Majesty will graciously pardon the liberty that I, a poor and at present forsaken widow, take in sending you my unworthy petition ...' Bugenhagen added a postscript endorsing what she had written. That was on the 8th January. On the 20th March a courier rode in with a gift and greetings from the King.

For some time now Katie's strength had been waning. When the warm weather came that summer, instead of health, it brought the plague once more to Wittenberg. The University was ordered to go to Torgau and Katie decided to go there too so out through the Elster Gate and past the summerhouse of happy memory they rode. As the wagon jolted along by the edge of a lake she was thrown out and was lifted out of the water stunned and bruised. When they arrived in Torgau Katie was ill. Chill and shock had brought on a fever. Casper Grünewald, who had been a close friend of Luther, opened his home to the family and gave the invalid every care but Katie never regained her health and during the next three months her strength gradually ebbed. She spoke much of Luther, awake and sleeping.

Winter came and the children anxiously tended her. Hans, now twenty-six, had been appointed a councillor of state to the Elector, John Frederick II. He in time married a daughter of Cruziger, his father's close friend. The younger children Katie had brought through their impressionable teenage years. Martin, who had always been rather delicate was twenty-one and studying theology. He married the daughter of a councillor of Wittenberg and died when thirty-two. Paul, almost twenty and the most gifted, became a doctor and, after a short spell as Professor of Medicine at the University of Jena, became a court physician to the Elector of Saxony at Dresden. It is of interest that he paid tribute to his mother's medical skill saying that she was half-way to being a doctor. Margaretha was eighteen on the 17th December. In 1555 she married George, the son of a Prussian nobleman, Albrecht von Kunheim, a great admirer of Luther, and went to live in East Prussia. They had nine children and in that land Margaretha was buried.

Katie developed pneumonia and the doctor held out little hope of recovery. By the afternoon of the 20th December it was obvious that her strength was failing. 'I will cleave to the Lord Christ,' she said, 'as the burr to the cloth.' As the evening wore on her children watched in silence as the mother who had worked so energetically for them slept on in weakness.

At about nine o'clock she woke and, seeing their tired faces, begged them to go to bed. 'See, I too am weary.' Gretchen helped to make her comfortable and she closed her eyes. An hour passed and Gretchen tiptoed to the bed to listen, but all was still. They had sent a saint to heaven. She was only fifty-three.

In sleep all weariness is laid aside and we become cheerful again, and rise in the morning fresh and well. So shall we awake from our graves in the last day, as though we had only slept a night, and bathe our eyes and rise fresh and well. Heaven and earth will be renewed, and we who believe shall be everywhere at home.

Martin Luther

MARTIN LUTHER

THE MAN WHO STARTED THE REFORMATION
Thomas Lindsay

Martin Luther
The Man who Started the Reformation
by Thomas Lindsay

ISBN: 978-1-85792-261-5

Martin Luther's father was a miner with ambitions – he wanted to better himself and provide his children with a good education. Martin upset his father's plan by becoming a monk rather than a lawyer, but by the age of twenty-nine he was a professor of theology. In addition to his college duties he preached almost every day and visited people on pastoral duties – he kept two secretaries very busy.

Luther's father, meanwhile, became a town councillor, the part owner of six mines and owned a large house in the main street.

What happened to make this son of the upwardly mobile establishment into the revolutionary who nailed 95 Theses onto the church door at Wittenberg, affecting not only the whole of the Christian church but also breaking the power of a European superstate? This is the story of a passionate, flawed and courageous man who loved his family and the people around him; a man who went further in challenging the status quo than any other in history, the man who started the Reformation.

CHRISTOPHER CATHERWOOD

FIVE LEADING REFORMERS

Lives at a watershed of history

MARTIN LUTHER
THOMAS CRANMER
JOHN CALVIN
JOHN KNOX
ULRICH ZWINGLI

*"Each in his way was a watershed figure, and Catherwood's vivid
profiling of them will help to keep their memory green."*
J. I. Packer

Five Leading Reformers
Lives at a Watershed of History

ISBN: 978-1-84550-553-0

Christopher Catherwood summarises the lives of Martin Luther, John Calvin, Ulrich Zwingli, Thomas Cranmer and John Knox. He unlocks the motivation, the power and drive that pushed these men to risk their position, their livelihoods and their lives.

GRACE
ESSENTIALS

BORN SLAVES
THE BONDAGE OF THE WILL

MARTIN LUTHER

GRACE ESSENTIALS
Born Slaves
The Bondage of the Will
by Martin Luther

ISBN: 978-1-78191-966-8

By grace alone, through faith alone – words no less relevant today than they were when Martin Luther first used them to shake the Roman Catholic church to its core. *The Bondage of the Will,* first published in 1525 and very possibly Luther's most famous work, argues against the idea that we choose salvation of our own free will. Born Slaves presents this work, retaining the distinctive style and voice of Luther, for a modern audience.

Christian Focus Publications

Our mission statement –

STAYING FAITHFUL
In dependence upon God we seek to impact the world through literature faithful to His infallible Word, the Bible. Our aim is to ensure that the Lord Jesus Christ is presented as the only hope to obtain forgiveness of sin, live a useful life and look forward to heaven with Him.

Our books are published in four imprints:

CHRISTIAN
FOCUS

Popular works including biographies, commentaries, basic doctrine and Christian living.

CHRISTIAN
HERITAGE

Books representing some of the best material from the rich heritage of the church.

MENTOR

Books written at a level suitable for Bible College and seminary students, pastors, and other serious readers. The imprint includes commentaries, doctrinal studies, examination of current issues and church history.

CF4•K

Children's books for quality Bible teaching and for all age groups: Sunday school curriculum, puzzle and activity books; personal and family devotional titles, biographies and inspirational stories – Because you are never too young to know Jesus!

Christian Focus Publications Ltd,
Geanies House, Fearn, Ross-shire,
IV20 1TW, Scotland, United Kingdom.
www.christianfocus.com